D0192952

Praise for *I Heart My Life*

'Emily is the stand-out leader for driven women who want to transform their lives by healing their mindset and money mindset.'

NIYC PIDGEON, POSITIVE PSYCHOLOGIST, CERTIFIED HIGH-PERFORMANCE AND SUCCESS COACH, AND BESTSELLING AUTHOR OF *NOW IS YOUR CHANCE*

'Emily Williams is a fearless champion for ambitious women who want more out of life. She's helped countless women leave their 9–5 jobs, start a business, and make more money than ever before. She is passionate, determined, and sincere – and won't let you settle for anything less than your biggest dreams!'

SELENA SOO, CREATOR OF IMPACTING MILLIONS

'If you're looking to master the inner game of wealth, look no further. Emily is direct – no B.S. – and one of the most sincere champions of your success I have ever met. She is full of love, but no fluff. Her commitment to helping women build epic businesses and brands will get you all the results you desire and more!'

SARAH KALER, LEADERSHIP COACH, SOULPOWERED.COM

'Emily truly helped me "flip the switch" on how I view money, freedom, and even fear itself.'

CHRIS WINFIELD, CREATOR OF UNFAIR ADVANTAGE LIVE AND COLUMNIST FOR INC.COM AND ENTREPRENUER.COM

I Heart my Life

I Heart My Life

Discover Your Purpose, Transform Your Mindset, and Create Success Beyond Your Dreams

EMILY WILLIAMS

HAY HOUSE
Carlsbad, California • New York City
London • Sydney • New Delhi

Published in the United Kingdom by:
Hay House UK Ltd, Astley House, 33 Notting Hill Gate, London W11 3JQ
Tel: +44 (0)20 3675 2450; Fax: +44 (0)20 3675 2451; www.hayhouse.co.uk

Published in the United States of America by:
Hay House Inc., PO Box 5100, Carlsbad, CA 92018-5100
Tel: (1) 760 431 7695 or (800) 654 5126; Fax: (1) 760 431 6948 or (800) 650 5115
www.hayhouse.com

Published in Australia by:
Hay House Australia Ltd, 18/36 Ralph St, Alexandria NSW 2015
Tel: (61) 2 9669 4299; Fax: (61) 2 9669 4144; www.hayhouse.com.au

Published in India by:
Hay House Publishers India, Muskaan Complex, Plot No.3, B-2,
Vasant Kunj, New Delhi 110 070
Tel: (91) 11 4176 1620; Fax: (91) 11 4176 1630; www.hayhouse.co.in

Text © Emily Williams, 2019

The moral rights of the author have been asserted.

All rights reserved. No part of this book may be reproduced by any mechanical, photographic or electronic process, or in the form of a phonographic recording; nor may it be stored in a retrieval system, transmitted or otherwise be copied for public or private use, other than for 'fair use' as brief quotations embodied in articles and reviews, without prior written permission of the publisher.

The information given in this book should not be treated as a substitute for professional medical advice; always consult a medical practitioner. Any use of information in this book is at the reader's discretion and risk. Neither the author nor the publisher can be held responsible for any loss, claim or damage arising out of the use, or misuse, of the suggestions made, the failure to take medical advice or for any material on third-party websites.

A catalogue record for this book is available from the British Library.

Hardcover ISBN: 978-1-78817-286-8
E-book ISBN: 978-1-78817-310-0
Audiobook ISBN: 978-1-78817-352-0

Certified Chain of Custody
Promoting Sustainable Forestry
www.sfiprogram.org
SFI-01268

SFI label applies to the text stock

To my husband James, who has supported me through every high and every low: You are my everything, and the real reason I now truly heart my life.

'Do not fear to be your true self, for everything you want wants you.'[1]

Genevieve Berhrand

Contents

Preface

The letter I wrote to myself on my 25th birthday

October, 2010

It's 4 a.m. and I can't sleep. Turning on my computer, I check out a few dating sites – there isn't much to do at this time of night, especially when you live alone. I quickly sign off when I start to get messages like, 'How cum ur still up? Cum to me in Battersea xx' and 'Morning Elo11, looking good. Are you awake?' I forgot that people can virtually see my presence on this particular site. Gross. Online dating is so weird. I never thought I'd be trying to meet someone this way.

Standing up, I switch on my lights, lie on my bed, and rearrange my body into work position. Over the next hour, I consider another wave of career choices – should I look for a part-time nanny job (it seems that's all you can get with a psychology degree)? – and weigh up my options for finding a new apartment. But wait, there's actually nothing I can afford. Never mind.

My stomach starts to knot up and tears stream down my cheeks. My sadness increases with the realization that nothing seems to be going right in my life. I'm beyond overwhelmed. Thoughts of frustration and questions live in my mind. They seem to have taken up a permanent home there, and more than anything, I want them to go away. I'm so sick of feeling lost and confused.

What do I want for my life? Certainly not this. I look around at the ugly, light-colored Ikea furniture that the rental agency chose to decorate this apartment. I barely own anything in this place. All of it is temporary and unsettled – fleeting – and it's all been used before. I want a place to call my own. I want to be able to afford the dark-colored furniture (is that more expensive or something?!) I want a kitchen (with an oven) that isn't 5 feet away from my bed. I want a washing machine, a television, and a bathtub.

I want a new home, where I won't have to listen to the guy upstairs stomping around his room early in the morning. Or hear him peeing when he gets home from work every day. Oh, except for Thursdays: he's off on Thursdays. I don't want vomit falling onto my bed at 1 a.m., after he decides to throw up out the window. (I thought it was rain at first, until I picked up my blanket and smelled it.)

And don't even get me started on my love life. I've scared off yet another man (this one only lasted two weeks) and have no other prospects. My ex won't speak to me, and has simply returned my clothes in the mail in a complete ball of mess. I don't know what I did to make him hate me. He didn't even write my surname on the address label – all it said was 'Emily.'

I guess I'm glad that everyone who has broken my heart did so, since they weren't right for me anyway, but that doesn't mean I'm less lonely. I want to find Him – the one – and go to the top of the Eiffel Tower. I've stood in front of it twice, but I never went up it. I decided almost

10 years ago that I wouldn't take the magical elevator ride up and look over the City of Light until I was with a man I loved. That seemed like the perfect scenario to me: little did I know I'd still be waiting.

As I blew out the candles on my cake at dinner (now eight hours ago), my wish was to find love this year. We'll see. I've made that wish every birthday since I can remember.

Hoping things get better soon,

Emily

In case it's not obvious, that girl did *not* heart her life. A few months earlier, she'd moved to London from Ohio in the United States. She'd had high hopes that, with a cross-Atlantic relocation, her life would improve. Her quarter-life crisis would end, and she'd get clarity on her purpose, become wildly rich, and find the love of her life.

That girl had been wishing her whole life: as a child, she'd set the alarm on her chunky G-star watch to go off at 11:11 (a lucky number) every morning, after which she'd make a wish; and when her parents took her on trips – from Florida to Italy – she'd wished when she threw coins into fountains.

She wanted a life that lit her up. A trip to the top of the Eiffel Tower, a bestselling book, her own business, a beautiful home (well, more like a mansion), true love, travel – she wanted all that life had to offer. And deep down, she knew she was meant for something big in this world. Meant to have an impact. Meant to shine.

I have compassion for that girl. This book is for her. And in case it's not obvious, she's not just me: she's you too. She's in all of us.

Introduction

Oprah Winfrey's commanding voice boomed from the speakers and the huge screen in front of us lit up with black-and-white images of her early life. It was 2014 and my father-in-law had paid for me to fly from London to Washington D.C. to attend Oprah's 'Live Your Best Life' event. Upon hearing our host's first words, the thousands of people in the audience stood up and cheered, immediately mesmerized.

She told us a story about her grandma, who had raised her in Mississippi, in the Deep South of the US, while working as a maid. One day, as she hung up wet laundry on the clothesline, she'd spoken softly to the young girl about her purpose in life: 'You have to watch me Oprah Gayle, because one day you'll have to do this for yourself.'[1]

Oprah knew well enough not to talk back to this beloved woman, but in her little girl mind, she knew that *wasn't* her purpose in life. Although she may have outwardly nodded as a sign of respect, she secretly shook her head simultaneously, knowing she was meant for more.

This early incident in Oprah's life illustrates just how powerful our gut instinct, heart, belief, intuition actually is (in this book,

I'll be using these terms interchangeably). Her mind couldn't have dreamt that: it was all heart. The feeling that she was meant for something big was what pulled her and directed her onto her path – to the success she's had over her lifetime – and it can do that for you too.

The Message I Was Born to Share

As a seven-figure entrepreneur, author, speaker, course creator, and success coach, I have the rare opportunity of seeing human success (and failure) firsthand, and I know what it *really* takes to achieve big goals. Every single day since starting my company, I Heart My Life (IHML), I've worked with driven women around the world.

I've seen them celebrate huge milestones: resigning from a 9–5 job; enabling their husband to quit his job and follow *his* dreams; the manifestation of trips; turning an annual salary into a monthly income; breaking harmful family patterns that have lasted for generations; an increase in confidence; and going after dreams they never thought they'd have the opportunity to reach.

But I've also seen a lack of awareness when it comes to desire. I've seen women deny what they want and allow their inner demons or fear to run the show. I've witnessed jealousy, stubbornness, and competition take women down. I've watched them question whether what they really want, deep within, is possible for them. And most painfully, I've seen them deny that they are worthy of the success they desire.

This book is about supporting women in getting clear about what it is they actually want, giving themselves permission to have it, and taking the steps required to obtain it. That means you too.

The message I've been put on this Earth to share with you is that *anything is possible*. You're capable of so much more than you know, and I'm in the business of helping you realize this and bring it to light.

During my own journey, there were two key moments when my life truly changed course, and I'll share these with you later in the book. Maybe this is one of those key moments for you. Whether you sought out this book or were gifted it by someone who loves you, I'm so glad our paths have crossed. I know that wasn't an accident, either – as you read on, you'll see that I believe everything happens for a reason.

You're meant for more and this is your time. Not living up to your full potential doesn't serve anyone: not you, not the world. It's time to stop playing small.

Stop Playing Small

Simply put: I believe the sky is the limit when it comes to your dreams, and right now, you're probably living a small fraction of what you're truly capable of. You're listening to what others deem is possible for you, instead of the internal barometer that is your heart. You're creating self-imposed limitations for your life and your success.

This book is an invitation to start showing up in a different way, and to truly live the life you were born for, maybe for the first time.

As the spiritual teacher and author Marianne Williamson says: 'Your playing small does not serve the world. There is nothing enlightened about shrinking so that other people won't feel insecure around you.[2]

The good news is that everything you desire is already within you. I'm certain of that. This is about you becoming the person you were meant to be. This is about you showing up. This is about you taking your life by the reins and no longer settling for 'good enough.' This is about you living an extraordinary life.

The Importance of Mindset

Maybe everything I've shared so far is starting to bring up red flags for you. *Who is this Emily Williams?* you might be thinking. *She doesn't know what's possible or not possible for me. Doesn't she realize that I'm not smart enough, rich enough, skinny enough* (insert your own 'enough' statement) *to get everything I desire?*

If that's the script currently running through your mind, or if you can hear other doubts creeping in, just know this is completely normal.

But what if I told you that you don't have to welcome every thought that comes into your mind, and that you don't have to believe every thought either? And what if I told you that, in order to create a life you love, you must monitor and transform your thoughts? You can't let just *anything* seep in. What if I told you that your mission from now on is to be fiercely protective of your mind, because it is the foundation for everything you can create?

Think about what it takes to build a home; I'm not a contractor, but even I know that you need to pick a plot of land that's suitable for building and then focus on creating a strong foundation. So many of us are building our lives, dreams, businesses, and careers on a shaky foundation: like a card deck about ready to topple over. But it doesn't have to be that way.

One of the reasons my clients are so successful is the deep work we do to create a strong foundation on which their dreams can grow. The plan is important, but if someone is lacking in confidence, courage, or even clarity, they aren't going to take the action needed to move forward with their dreams. So, first of all, you have to get really clear about *your* foundation. What are you building your house on? Is it stable ground or quicksand? We'll uncover the answer together, but for now – for the next few pages at least – tell those doubts to take a back seat, because you're driving.

Implementation

Speaking of driving, this book is also about you *taking action*. I know there can be a lot of questions and confusion when you're going for your dreams and transforming your life. Without guidance and support, it can be difficult to make any progress at all. That's why I'll be showing you the *exact steps* you need to take to get there – those that have worked for my clients and for me. My goal is that by the time you reach the end of this book, you won't even recognize your own life because so much will have changed and shifted.

But please, know that it's not enough to just *read* this book. We've been conditioned to scan, memorize, and repeat, but that's not going to get you the life you want. One of my former mentors, multimillion-dollar entrepreneur, author, speaker, and coach Brendon Burchard, has a fabulous saying that illustrates this beautifully: 'Common sense isn't always common practice, which is why so many potentially great people suffer.'[3]

Your goal is to take action on everything that I teach you in this book, and to integrate what I teach you into your life – not just read these words. You may put your own spin on it (in fact, you should, because you are your own, unique person), but taking action is key to creating success.

How to Use the Book

Here's how I recommend you approach the book – both to get the most from it and to start to immediately see huge shifts in your life:

1. Be Open

I'm going to share with you concepts that you've probably never heard about before. Be open to them working for you. Don't discount anything. Although you may find that not everything resonates with you or works for you right now, it can and it will, over time.

For example, every time I work with a coach, there are elements of our work together that sink in immediately and others that come to light when I'm ready at some point in the future. Trust that all is unfolding as it's meant to and that you're hearing what you need to hear.

2. Journal

Use a journal alongside this book and as you go through each chapter, really study the words and take notes. Also, every chapter features a Success Tip and ends with an Action Step, and *I want you to complete all of them*. If you want to stop settling for a life that doesn't light you up, make these non-negotiable. *Nothing will change unless you do*. Let this be the change. And by the way, they are simple and meant to be fun!

3. Trust Your Inner Knowing

What I've come to realize over the past few years, through working with thousands of women around the world, is that most people are in denial about what they're meant for. And maybe that's you right now. I invite you to start to trust and know that today doesn't dictate what's possible for you tomorrow – and neither does the shape of your body, your bank account, or your high-school SAT score.

Whatever you want, it's possible for you to have it. If you can envision it, you can have it. Simple as that. Trust your inner knowing and bring that feeling to the surface. If you believe you're meant for more, then you are!

4. Make a Decision

How about we decide here and now that *this* is the moment your whole life changes course? You can choose to do that *right now*. The word 'decide' literally means 'to cut off' so let's cut off any possibility that you're meant for anything less than extraordinary.

Today, ask yourself what you want for your life. Heck, what do you want for your week? How are you holding yourself back? What are you longing for? What do you need to start believing is possible for you? No more excuses. Your dream life starts with this decision.

5. Be Selfish

As women, our programming is still along the lines of 'give to others and leave yourself with the crumbs.' If that's where you're at today, please know that you can give to others *and* go for your dreams. And in fact, going for your dreams is the best thing you can do for others.

You doing this work and creating your most successful life is a gift for them, too! They get to see what's possible and that will open their own mindset to possibility and change. If you have children, think about the example you'll be setting for them. Think about what they're going to see you accomplish, and in turn, feel that you gave them permission to do what they desire too. What a gift!

6. Know That No One Is Coming

At the same time, know that doing this for others cannot be your own motivation. I know, you want to be selfless, altruistic, win a prize for how much you give to others and put yourself last, but I beg you to start thinking of yourself and your own happiness. No one else is going to put you and your dreams first.

As motivational speaker and bestselling author Mel Robbins says in her book *The 5 Second Rule*, 'No one is coming. It is up to you. It has always been and will always be up to you.'[4] I want you to truly understand that this is your time and this is your chance. We get one life. Stop being a victim, stop complaining, stop pretending that you're happy when you're not. I can help you. *Allow* me to help you. We can do this together.

7. See Yourself in Others

Throughout our journey, I'll be providing insights from my own life and my clients' experiences. Each chapter starts with an extract of my journey between 2008 and 2018. Then I've woven some of my clients' stories into each chapter, along with stories about other influential people and experts whom I've studied with and learned from over the years.

The reason I've done this is because our behavior is learned through stories and by watching others take the action we desire (whether we know we desire it or not). For example, when you were a young child, you saw your parents or older siblings walking and learned to do it yourself. Although some behavior is rooted in instinct, much of what we experience and do in life results from seeing others do it. Understanding that it's possible for us gives us the confidence to also give it a shot.

One of the scientific reasons behind this is a distinctive class of neurons in our brain called mirror neurons. Firing off when we take action, as well as when we observe someone else taking the same or a similar action, mirror neurons explain why when we see or hear someone yawn, *we* yawn.[5]

The same thing happens when you hear stories of success and triumph. Sara Blakely, Mark Zuckerberg, Richard Branson… these and all the other people who are doing something new and great. We know it's possible because they've showed us how.

As you're reading along, I ask that you try to see yourself in these stories. In other words, see yourself doing what we did. And if you don't believe what I've done is possible for you, think about it like this: I'm human, you're human, so whatever I've done is possible for you too. For instance, would you walk past me sitting in my First Class seat on a plane and tell me that it isn't physically possible for you to sit in First Class too? You are capable of moving from 23B to 1A; trust me, I did it! (You can adopt *my belief in you* if you don't yet have that self-belief available for yourself.)

8. Be Kind to Yourself

You, too, have so much to give, so much potential to reach. You're capable of more than you know, and so much is possible for you. And it all starts with loving *you* and being kind to yourself. Success is not about being critical or mean to yourself – it's about loving yourself like your life depends on it (because it does).

9. Know This Won't Be Easy

The work you'll undertake in this book is going to change your life. To be able to say that you don't even recognize your own life means we're going to be doing a pretty extensive overhaul of what currently exists. And, as with any overhaul – digging up the dirt, stretching into possibility, and reaching new heights – it doesn't come without some pain at times.

Think of the process as like giving birth to a new life. There will be uncomfortable moments – contractions – but it will be so worth it in the end. And just like a new life coming to this Earth, in those challenging moments you can celebrate. The growth is happening. Changes are taking place. You wouldn't feel any of those things unless you were growing, so it's good news! And the other good news is that I'm going to show you how to handle those moments. I'm going to show you how to have far more exciting and positive moments – even *pinch me* ones.

10. Celebrate

When it comes to celebrating, my friend and fellow Hay House author Niyc Pidgeon says, 'There's evidence to show that when you celebrate your strengths, you become stronger and more successful. People actually build better relationships with you,

you reach your goals so much faster, and you're physically and mentally healthier as well. It's not just a women's empowerment thing, but a scientific thing as well.'[6]

For that reason, in all of our programs at IHML, we have a tradition of celebrating with Success Fridays. Our clients share that week's successes, and explain what they're proud of or excited by. I want you to do the same as you read the book, so I've included Celebration Breaks in every chapter. When you come to one, take a few minutes to complete it. It's there for a reason, not just to look pretty.

Reality Check

I'm well aware that many of the opportunities and luxuries I present in this book are not available to every woman on the planet. At least not yet. I recognize that a huge percentage of the world's population doesn't have the opportunity to make big life decisions or follow their heart. I hope that I see that change in my lifetime, and I will do everything in my power to continue to inspire diverse groups of people and foster change in the world.

For the purposes of this book, I'm going to focus on women who *are* able to go for their dreams. Those of us who have the right to choose; the right to follow our desires; the right to make as much money as we wish. I want to remind you that we owe it to ourselves and to the women out there without that freedom, to finally take the reins and create a life better than our dreams. We have a choice, and that, in itself, is miraculous.

I ask that you don't squander that choice any longer. We can choose to live a life that's less than what we desire – a life of 'almosts' and 'could haves' – or we can choose to go after our dreams and live an extraordinary life. Otherwise, we're spitting in the face of those who fought so hard for us to have the rights we have today. We're wasting our one precious life, and we have to ask ourselves what other less privileged women around the world would say to that – those who dream of going to university, marrying someone they actually love, becoming a doctor, or starting their own business; the ones who dream of deciding how many kids they want to have.

What would they say? What would they do with the opportunities that you have? Lovely, if you can't do it for you, do it for them.

The View from Where I Sit Today

Nearly eight years have passed since I wrote that letter to myself on my 25th birthday, and today, as I look out at the Duomo in Florence, Italy (where I'm writing this book), I wonder how I got here. How did I end up living in London, meeting the man of my dreams online, running a seven-figure company, and writing this book in a 5-star luxury Italian hotel for a woman like you? How does that even happen?

After years of learning from the best coaches, teachers, and leaders, and in personally coaching women all around the world to make *their* dreams a reality, I know the answer is simple: follow your heart.

The book *A Course in Miracles* reinterprets the biblical quote 'Many are called, but few are chosen' as 'All are called, but few choose to listen.'[7] To that, I'd like to add: 'Many are called, but few choose to listen and take action.' You're called for something big. You're called for the life you want. It's time to act.

In the pages that follow, I'm going to teach you the principles that will make you wildly successful. I'm going to show you how to create more wealth in your life, drop the limitations that are holding you back, and finally have all the secrets you've been craving when it comes to going for your dreams. But it all comes down to following your heart. That's all it's ever really about.

And remember, I'm just a girl from Ohio with really big dreams: if I can create a life *better* than my dreams, so can you. Let's do this!

Join the I Heart My Life Movement

This isn't just a book – it's a movement. A movement of women who are done settling for a life that doesn't light them up; women who know they're meant for something big, and are achieving it; women who are creating success beyond their dreams. This is your invitation to join them. Here's how:

1. Read the book and complete the Success Tips, Celebration Breaks, and Action Steps in each chapter.

2. Join me on www.iheartmylife.com. There, you can become a member and hear about our live events and courses.

3. Spread the word. One of my favorite things is to gift friends and family books that have impacted my life, in the hope that they will have the same experience. If you know someone who would love the stories, concepts, and messages in this book, please gift her a copy. After all, sometimes we choose a book, and other times, it chooses us.

CHAPTER 1

Belief

'Create the highest, grandest vision possible for your life, because you become what you believe."[1]

OPRAH WINFREY

In April 2008, toward the end of my senior year in college, I learned that I'd been accepted into 10 out of the 12 graduate schools to which I'd applied the previous year. San Francisco, Colorado, North Carolina, Chicago, New York; I had the United States covered and flew to lots of cities to get a feel for their campuses, programs, and staff.

Upon finally making a decision, I called the Program Director at Northwestern University in Chicago and told her I planned to make her school my home for the next three years. She was welcoming and comforted me in my decision, saying, 'Make sure to let your parents know we'll take good care of you.' I smiled to myself and thanked her.

And yet, soon after that phone call, something started to shift. Throughout those next few months, I enjoyed being in my home state of Ohio more than I'd anticipated, and the idea of leaving felt off. This came as a huge surprise to me, seeing that all year long – in fact, all life long – I'd wanted to get out of there.

I knew there was nothing for me in the city of Columbus (except for my family and friends, of course), and I was ready to leave; but I began to freak out and wondered what I was really doing with my life and if my future career plans were the right ones. For the first time, I started to worry about the seriousness of life after college.

Was I ready to spend another three years in school and take out more than $100,000 in student loans? Did I want to leave the only friends I'd ever known? It was all very daunting, but I chalked it up to something similar to pre-wedding jitters and continued to move forward and make plans for the move (ignoring the doubts that had started to surface).

The time came to find an apartment in the city that I would soon call my home. Two hours into the five-hour ride from Columbus to Chicago, with my mom driving, I found my heart rising into my throat with every passing town. I swallowed hard, in the hope that it would contain the emotions I was holding inside. Tears began to form in my eyes, beneath my favorite oversized sunglasses, but I quickly wiped them away – just as I'd done dozens of times before when I wanted to hide any sign of weakness.

But mothers always know. 'It doesn't seem like your heart is really into this,' my mom commented. She'd interrupted my thoughts about that summer, and wanting to get back to Columbus in time to go to a friend's softball game. I'm sure she'd noticed my tears too. 'Something has changed. Is it the money?' she asked.

'I don't know, Mom,' I replied. I truly didn't.

'I just don't know anything anymore,' I continued. 'I need time to think. I need a few weeks. Maybe we can come back next month and look for a place? There would still be time at that point...'

I waited for her response, but it never came, at least not in the form of words. Instead, she turned the car around.

I never did move to Chicago, and that was the first moment my whole life changed course.

Meant for 'Something Big'

Meant for something big. Meant for something big. Meant for something big. Do you hear that? It often starts as a whisper; then, just as a flame does if you tend to it and cultivate it, that whisper becomes louder. You become braver. You start to take action. Doors open.

I've heard that whisper since I was a young girl, and given that you're reading this book, you can probably relate to what I'm saying. That whisper comes to you at work – when you're sitting in the cubicle at 7 p.m., wondering when you're going to get to go home so you can spend your time doing what you really want to do. It comes to you when you pass the bookstore and imagine the cover of your own book staring out through the window. It comes to you when you see your friends taking a trip to Bali and feel a pang of jealousy that you're not under the verdant palm trees with them. It comes to you when you feel the calling to move to a new city, despite not knowing anyone there.

You probably also feel different. You don't fit in with your family or your group of friends; they don't get you. They think your head is in the clouds and that you should just be grateful for what you have. But you know the truth: you're meant for something big. You're meant for more. And just like I realized in the car on that drive to Chicago, and just like Oprah Winfrey realized as a young child in that story in the Introduction, your current reality and life right now are most definitely not all that's in store for you.

Why We Deny Our Something Big

I've come to realize over the past few years that most people are in denial about what they're meant for. There are women who'll tell you that they don't hear a calling at all, but don't be fooled by them. It's there, whether they can hear it or not – it's just that in those moments, the sound is disguised: like one of those whistles that only dogs can hear. Those who can't hear their calling simply haven't tuned in enough to themselves and their own heart and intuition, so they miss it.

Similarly, there are people who definitely hear the calling, but they push it away. They are ashamed of the whisper and scared of what it means for them and about them. Much like the tears you hold back when the date doesn't go as planned, when your boss yells at you in the meeting, or when your parents ask how you're feeling, you hold back the whisper. You pretend it isn't there and assure the world that everything's fine as it is. You do that in order to fit in. To avoid rocking the boat. To stay safe.

If you've denied your 'something big' in the past – or if you're doing it now – just know that there's nothing wrong with you. Simply put: up until now, you couldn't help it. The truth is, you've been programmed not to show up for years.

Maybe you know you're meant for something big but you hear the louder voices of your family, society, or even yourself saying you should just be grateful for what you have, and those voices overpower the whisper. They remind you that if you don't ever put yourself out there, you won't fail – and that feels, well, much safer than failing.

The issue is that most of us don't actually know this is happening beneath the surface. We hear the whisper of 'something more' and almost simultaneously hear what we deem to be the 'voice of reason' – reminding us that we don't have the money to start the business; that we haven't been with the company long enough to ask for the raise; or that we don't deserve the love of the man.

My darling friend, that is *not* the voice of 'reason' – that's the voice of fear and old programming, and it's essential you learn to call it like it is and stop believing it. That voice is going to come up throughout this book, and I'm going to teach you exactly how to handle it. But first, think about that calling or whisper. Are you in denial? Are you listening? Are you ready to answer the call? It's time.

The Lure of Safety

When I was young, as the oldest child and first-born girl, my parents were very protective of me. Even as a senior in high school, my curfew was never later than 11 p.m. I wasn't allowed to go to the boy/girl sleepover after prom or be alone in the basement for very long with a boy I was dating. Even when my husband James and I were engaged, we had to stay in separate rooms on family trips or when we visited my parents.

Looking back, I have compassion for those rules. Although I hated them at the time, I can see that my parents just wanted to keep me safe. They were using all the knowledge they'd been given from their parents and their parents' parents to make decisions about the wellbeing of their own children.

It's the same with that voice you hear on a regular basis: telling you not to take action, that you're not good enough, or that things won't work out – safety is its only concern. Some people refer to that voice as the ego or the subconscious, and I use both terms interchangeably. What you need to know is that your ego exists to keep you alive, but it is also a fear-based voice inside that wants to hold you back. It's doing the best it can, but it doesn't like change.

In fact, it deems all change unsafe. This work that we're going to do together is about reprogramming your mind (you'll learn how to do that later, and we'll dive deeper into this concept of safety) and taking new action on behalf of your dreams in a way you've never done before.

You've been programmed not to show up for years.

Success Tip

Look around. Feel the safety that exists for you today. In this moment, while you're reading this book, allow all your worries to disappear. You can continue this practice of bringing yourself back to the present moment and your present safety whenever your mind brings up new fears and doubts.

Hunters and Gatherers

So, why have you been playing it safe? Although we're no longer hunters and gatherers like our ancient ancestors, and many of us no longer live in the same village as our family from birth to death, there remain quite a few tendencies that have been passed down from hundreds (and thousands) of years ago.

From an evolutionary perspective, there was a time when the human race needed to stay within the box in order to survive. We needed to make sure people liked us. We couldn't deviate from the path (literally) because our community equaled safety. We had to stay within the group, otherwise we wouldn't have the food and shelter we required to survive and could even be attacked or killed.

As you can clearly see, for those of us in the Western world, this is not our current reality. Most of us are safe. Yet every day, we're making decisions with default programming that tells us we're not. We stay in the 'safe' job; we get married to the 'safe' partner; we avoid using credit cards because they are 'unsafe.' We haven't learned to update our own programming. (And why would we? This isn't taught in school.)

We're still functioning with an old operating system that's detrimental to our success.

Think about it like this: would you expect a computer retrieved from Apple founder Steve Job's garage in the 70s to work properly today, and give you the results you want? Of course not – you're way too smart for that. But your mind tells you that updates, reboots, and anything outside the norm are unsafe; and the reality is, you've been stuck believing it.

The ironic thing is, there's just as much to be afraid of *inside* the box (maybe even more!) Right now, you're settled, and walking around pretending to be happy. Saying you're fine with the way things are turning out. Denying the fact that you want to travel, enjoy luxury experiences, make more money, have an impact in the world – the list goes on. Yet you're hoping that happiness will be hand-delivered to you someday, along with opportunity, right to your front door.

You've been brainwashed to believe that you'll be in your 'safe' 9–5 job forever (yet all around you people are getting laid off or quitting due to burnout or depression). Is that really safe? And more importantly, is that really what you want? All that denial sounds (and is) exhausting. I say this with love and respect: unless something drastic changes, you're going to remain stuck forever.

We both know that it's time for you to figure out what you really want and make it happen. And to do that, it's essential that you follow your whispers.

Forget the 'How'

Now, you might be saying, 'Emily, that's great, but how? I don't have clarity – I've no clue what that "something big" actually is.' That's the part that trips you up. That's the part that makes you doubt everything you feel and causes you to push the whispers away. That's the part that makes you feel stuck, lost, confused, and even a little crazy.

All I ask of you right now is to put the 'how' to one side. That may sound counterintuitive – you'd never travel across the United States without your Google Maps app and a plan, so why would your goals be any different, right? Well, that's half correct, and we'll revisit this point later in the book. But for now, don't worry about having a specific destination. All I want is for you to acknowledge the whispers today. (And by the way, that step alone is more than most people do their entire lifetime, so you're already ahead of the game!)

Celebration Break

Celebrate the fact that you're already on the path to your most successful life, just by acknowledging your whispers!

Fireball

If it's any comfort, you should know that I've been in that place of confusion too! Do you think I knew my next steps when my mom turned that car around? No! Despite my success today, for a long time I had no real, tangible information about what I was meant for. In fact, even when James met me back in 2011 (three years *after* turning the car around), he said he could see this fireball inside of me. Neither of us knew what it was meant to be used for, but it was there, and I just needed to figure out what direction to point it in.

That directionless fireball still comes up from time to time today – when I'm itching to start on a new project or craving more clarity. We'll get into your specific fireball in the next few chapters (it's another piece that you may have buried, but it's there), but you don't actually have to know what your something big is yet. You can just know that it exists. It's your truth. It's meant for you. It's been there since the day you were born.

And the incredible thing is that it's not about a one-size-fits-all something big. It's about discovering what excites you, what you were put on this Earth to do; it's about your purpose, the life you're meant to live and what's unique to you. Right now, all I want you to do is bring that feeling to the surface. Reignite it if you've lost it. No longer deny what you're meant for.

The first step to creating a life you love is acknowledging that you're meant for something big.

For you, maybe that first step is a huge leap. Maybe it means so much more than that acknowledgment – it means potentially cutting ties with unsupportive family and friends or even a spouse. We don't need to go there yet, but I want to be really honest about what it takes to make your dreams a reality, and let you know that yes, dramatic changes are a real possibility.

But when you think about it – is there really another option? Do you want to get to the end of your life and question whether you've really lived? Or worse, regret not going for your dreams? I don't know of anyone who, on reaching the end of their life, said: 'I'm so glad I was practical. I'm so glad I didn't take that trip. I'm so glad I did the same thing day after day. I'm so glad I didn't follow my heart.' I don't want that to be you.

Miracles

In the book *A Course in Miracles*, it says that 'if miracles aren't naturally occurring in your life, then something has gone greatly wrong.'[2] I had no idea of this, did you? Miracles are meant to be natural occurrences, and you acknowledging your something big is the way you activate this. The desires in your heart are meant for you – whether they're to start a business, live abroad, become a millionaire, work with someone you admire, or speak around the world at live events with an audience of thousands. All of that is valid and meant for you, if that's what you want.

The reality is that your denying the whisper that says you're meant for something big isn't serving anyone, and it's *stunting* the miracles. As Marianne Williamson says: 'Our deepest fear is that we are powerful beyond measure. It is our light, not our darkness that most frightens us.'[3]

Have you ever thought of it that way? That it's a fear of living your 'something big' and shining your light that's actually scaring you and keeping you stuck in your tracks? Well, as my friend Rebecca Campbell says, 'Light is the new black.'[4] Light is everything. So, stick with me. I'm going to teach you how to move past that fear so you can shine just as you were born to do.

Action Step

Say these words out loud: 'I'm meant for something big.' Feel all the emotions that come with that statement, and then journal about what's coming up for you. Do you believe that statement is true? If not, what's stopping you from *really* believing it?

CHAPTER 2

Possibility

'We simply do not have time anymore to think so small.'[1]

ELIZABETH GILBERT

I'm blessed to have been brought up by parents who truly did believe that anything was possible for their children. They encouraged us to find out what really drove us and lit us up. I was taught things like 'do what you love, and the money will follow.' At Christmas my parents gave us books like The 7 Habits of Highly Effective Teenagers, The Purpose Driven Life *and* Chicken Soup for the Soul, *so personal development and the betterment of one's self was always a part of my reality.*

But after I gave up my spot at Northwestern University and stayed in Ohio, I was depressed and stuck and felt like a failure. I didn't have the clarity I was longing for and my life didn't resemble anything I wanted. I was confused about how I'd ended up in that place. Was I dreaming too big? Was I being silly, or unrealistic? What was wrong with me? I couldn't see the possibilities. Everything was cloudy.

For a while I worked at Starbucks (I had to apply three times before I actually got the job!), then at the local children's hospital. I even took chemistry classes, thinking I wanted to become a doctor. (That was short-lived – I actually left my Quarter 1 chemistry final in tears, knowing that it wasn't for me.)

All I could do was hope that my heart hadn't led me astray. There had to have been some reason I'd turned the car around, right?

If that's where you're at today – living a life that you no longer recognize, or waiting for your life to get good – it's crucial to understand that your current reality isn't your forever reality. Your present circumstances are no indication of what's possible for you. You have to continue to hold tight to your inner knowing that anything and everything is possible, because it is. So, regardless of how you grew up or what your current reality looks like, this chapter is about expanding your belief in *possibility*.

Imagine the Impossible

'We went to the Moonnnnnnnn!!!' Brendon Burchard screamed from the stage during his 'High Performance Academy Live' event in September 2016. James and I were in the audience, and just like the rest of the room, we burst out laughing as we watched the theatrics before us.

Brendon was so right. We went to the Moon! We defied all the odds, yet for some reason, we make building a business, going for our dreams, creating a website, asking for a raise, 'hard.' We stay inside the box and focus on what seems realistic. It's like we were given a Realistic Handbook in childhood that we're meant to abide by.

Yet if you look around, more people than ever before are breaking down barriers, inventing new products, traveling the world, and becoming millionaires – and at a younger age.[2] We all have the ability to create our own reality. And yet…

Most people are asleep at the wheel of life and don't realize that opportunities are there for the taking.

Most of us are addicted to 'realistic' without knowing that realistic focuses on restrictions – it basically says that you should just be happy with what you have, that your dreams aren't possible, and that aiming high will only lead to disappointment.

I entirely disagree with that approach. Telling yourself to 'be realistic' doesn't empower you – it doesn't inspire you to aim high, or to explore possibilities, or to dream big dreams. And who truly wants to live life like that? Is that even really living? I don't think so.

Anything Can Happen

At the outset of our IHML courses, we ask our students to imagine that anything can happen. Specifically, we invite them to do a brain dump of what their 'anything can happen' wildest dreams consist of. The point of this exercise is to get the juices flowing and to engage the imagination and heart and silence the ego (the voice inside that puts limits on us and our dreams).

Even if you don't see yourself as capable of achieving your wildest dreams, you don't have to look very far to see cases of regular people doing extraordinary things. For example, not so long ago, it was believed impossible for a human to run a mile in less than four minutes – there was a concept of 'a four-minute barrier' that couldn't be broken.

But then, in 1954, the British sprinter Roger Bannister proved everyone wrong by running a mile in three minutes 59.4 seconds, setting a world record. And the funny thing is, his record was broken just 46 days later, and many other athletes began to run sub-four-minute miles shortly thereafter.[3] As you can imagine, it wasn't a sudden change in human physical capability that made this a reality – it was a change in the perception of what was possible.

And of course, we don't need to go back to 1954 or to 1969 and the first Moon walk to see stories of human potential – we have modern-day superhero tales featuring people like Sara Blakely (founder of Spanx and in 2012 the youngest self-made female billionaire), Mark Zuckerberg (founder of Facebook), and Jeff Bezos (founder of Amazon) to name just a few. My point? Greatness is all around, and it's possible for you too.

When you let yourself dream 'unrealistically' big dreams in spite of what other people may tell you, not only will you knock your own socks off, you'll also be showing everyone around you what's possible, and we all know the world needs a new version of a reality check.

Success Tip

Try this exercise yourself right now: put on a timer for five minutes and brain dump a list of your wildest dreams. Don't censor yourself; in fact, challenge yourself to dream even bigger.

Reignite Your Imagination

The truth is, even if someone else hasn't done what you desire to do, it's still possible! Think about the smartphone or the Internet – neither of those technologies seemed possible, but with imagination they were brought to fruition.

Albert Einstein said that 'imagination is more important than knowledge. Knowledge is limited. Imagination encircles the world.[4] Einstein believed that in order to increase the intelligence of our children, we should tell them more fairytales. Now, I don't know about you but there are a lot of people out there who believe we should tell our children *fewer* fairytales. That they shouldn't grow up believing in things that aren't realistic. They shouldn't have their head in the clouds. They shouldn't get their hopes up.

Now even I can see the value of a little girl not relying on that prince on a white horse to save her, and maybe you feel that way too. But I don't think that's what Einstein was talking about. This is about using your imagination to create the life you desire – whatever that may be. Everything that is now real was once imagined, and that's incredible when you think about it.

Dr. Wayne Dyer, one of my favorite authors, illustrated this beautifully when he said: 'Everything that you can experience with your senses was once in someone else's imagination.'[5] So that iPhone you're holding, the computer you're working from, the home you're living in, the Uber you request every day, the train you travel to work on – all of these were at one point imagined. And if those things can be imagined, what's stopping you from imagining your perfect life? You should be able to, right?

But the reality is that most people have been taught that dreaming too big is wrong and dangerous, and that we're setting ourselves up for disappointment by living in that space. My goal is to help you reignite your imagination, and it starts with possibility.

Success Tip

Look around the room you're in right now. Which of the things in it were once imagined? Allow that to inspire you today.

Possibility and the Universal Laws

Let's take a look at possibility from the perspective of the Universal Laws. You're probably very familiar with the Physical Laws – the Law of Gravity or the Law of Motion – from science class as a child or teen. However, most of us don't learn about the Spiritual Laws, which are governed by the Universal Laws and are concerned with energy. Because they technically can't be seen, most people discount the Universal Laws, or just don't learn about them while growing up.[6]

As with the Law of Gravity, which you quickly came to believe in as a child when you realized you couldn't fly, putting the Universal Laws into practice is key, because you're a spiritual and energetic being having a physical experience and you need to know how to work with them to create ease, flow, and transformation in your life. We aren't going to spend too much time here, but I do want you to understand some key elements of the Universal Laws.

The most well known of the Universal Laws is the Law of Attraction, which you may have heard of. This states that you'll attract into your life whatever you're offering vibrationally – in other words, you get what you're focused on. The Law of Attraction is just one of many Universal Laws, however; the Law I'll be covering most in this book is the Law of Polarity, which will help you understand how anything you desire is possible for you – *even if you don't physically see it in your life this second.*

The Law of Polarity

The website TheLawOfAttraction.com states that 'according to the Law of Polarity, everything is dual – so things that appear to be opposites are actually two inseparable parts of the same thing. Think of hot and cold... although they're opposites, they're actually on the same continuum and you cannot have one without the potential for the other.'[7]

So when it comes to your desires, wealth, and the life you want to create, there may have been a period of time when, for example, you couldn't afford to take that dream trip; yet, in terms of your *potential*, if you can't do something, it means you *can* do something at the same time.

According to the Law of Polarity, you can't have a back without a front, or a yes without a no, or be broke without wealth being around the corner. Neither would exist without the other. You wouldn't know what dark was unless light existed, right? Would you know what wealth was unless you had something to compare it to? No! Therefore both exist together in the world and in your life.

I also think about the Law of Polarity in terms of human potential in general, because sometimes it's easier to see possibility in others before we see it in ourselves. For example, before I ever stayed in a 5-star hotel, I knew they existed and that they were often fully booked, so someone must be staying in them. Someone must be enjoying the drinks from the mini bar (otherwise, why would they put them in hotel rooms?) So, even though I wasn't yet staying in luxury hotels, I knew it was *possible* for me, even before the money was in the bank.

I focused on the fact that even though some of my desires weren't my current reality, there were people out there doing them all the time, so the *potential* was there for humans in general. And since I'm human, that meant the potential was there for me too. (That's where my 'why not me?' philosophy comes from; if someone is out there doing something you want to do, just ask yourself, *Why not me?* You'll start to see that there's no valid reason you can't do it, or have it, too!)

I hope this is sinking in for you today. What I'm saying is: even if you don't have everything you desire this second, it can be right around the corner because it literally already exists!

Celebration Break

I think the fact that everything you desire is already in existence deserves a Celebration Break. Let's do it!

Shift Your Attitude

The Titan Summit is a gathering of some of the world's best international speakers and thought leaders. The event is hosted by Robin Sharma – a huge presence in the coaching and personal development space – and is attended by billionaires and successful, driven people.

At one of the Titan Summits I attended, I met Lisa Bentley, a triathlete who at the time of writing, who has competed in 33 Ironman triathlons and won 11 of them. This would be an impressive accomplishment for anyone, but when you consider that Lisa has cystic fibrosis, it's a miracle.

During her presentation to the audience, Lisa shared something that really stood out for me: she said that one of the major things she'd recognized throughout her experience is that *attitude is more important than fact*. For example, even though she was aware that some of her competitors were (on paper) better sprinters, swimmers, and so on, she didn't put stock in those 'facts.' Instead, she focused on believing that anything was possible for her.

Lisa reminded herself to think the best of her capabilities, and to aim to be the very best version of herself. She declared that a true champion finds success *despite* adversity, and that so much of our success relies on retraining our brain to truly believe that anything is possible.

To me, Lisa's story is such an important illustration of the power of the mind when we put it to good use and stop believing the perceived limitations and 'facts' around us. Your attitude and thoughts truly do have the power to shape your reality and your future, in ways that will enable you to exceed expectations and falsify those facts. Lisa put it best when she said that you have to be your own biggest fan.

You need to cultivate an attitude that anything is possible, and that your desires for your future have no limit.

You need to trust that you have what it takes to make big things happen in your life, regardless of your current reality or what the 'facts' are telling you.

You're More Capable Than You Know

As Robin Sharma has often said: 'We were born into genius, but we were hypnotized into mediocrity.'[8] Meaning that we're all born as big dreamers with a limitless concept of what's possible for our lives, but along the way our social circle tells us that we're dreaming too big or that we need to 'face the facts.' But here's the good news: those 'facts' don't have to limit you any longer.

We're far more capable than we're willing to give ourselves credit for. We stop too soon; we hit the pause button; we slow down when things get just a little too tough. No, this isn't meant to make you feel bad: it's just meant to help you raise the bar on your own capabilities.

One of my favorite stories of mental strength and possibility concerns Ross Edgley, the 'World's Fittest Strongman,' who spent 157 days (or five months) swimming around the UK, being in the water for 12 hours each day. Ross is a scientist at heart who studies human performance and is obsessed with mental capability.

He claims that we're only using 40 percent of our potential when we stop doing something.[9] This means that, when it comes to the workout that feels impossible, the business deal that feels too risky, the video that you think you can't film and deliver, you actually have 60 percent more willpower that you can access to make those a reality! In other words, your mind has been programmed to stop at 40 percent.

Ross explains that this reaction – to quit when things get difficult – is a primitive mechanism that's meant to protect us from harm because the human body likes comfort and will try and keep us at the habitual level where everything is 'okay.'[10] (We'll look at this topic in more depth in the Mindset chapter.)

The truth is we all have a lot more in us that we think. (I mean, this is a guy who swam miles with a jellyfish on his face without even realizing it!) I see this all the time in my industry (in a less extreme way). For example, I've had coaches who had lost their business and gone bankrupt, but rebuilt and got back to the seven-figure mark just one year later; I've seen a coach speak on stage nine hours per day for five days straight with a broken

What if 'realistic' isn't meant to be your default setting?

foot; I've seen my clients overcome divorce, emotional abuse, drugs, alcohol, and self-harm. *Anything is possible.*

I'm not asking you to do any of those things (or swim 1,791 miles like Ross Edgley) – I'm asking you to go for your dreams. I'm asking you to raise the bar when it comes to possibility, to not stop right away, to keep going.

The Sky's the Limit

So, if the sky *were* the limit (and it is), what would you want? What would your perfect life or reality consist of? What's the new normal that you want to create? What if everything you desire to create, be, or do in your life (maybe all imagined at this moment) could also become real? Did you ever think about it that way? What if 'realistic' isn't meant to be your default setting?

What if you're capable of more, and by not using your imagination, you're actually holding yourself back from everything you're really meant for? What if you began to use your imagination every day? What if you envisioned the life you want and believed it was possible for you and meant for you, instead of shutting it down? (By the way, you can still show gratitude for what you're experiencing now and at the same time, desire more. We'll cover that later on in the book.) What if you believed that everything you wanted was already on its way to you?

I'm trying to get your wheels turning – is it working yet? It's time to reignite your imagination if the flame has gone out; to allow yourself to dream; to decide what it is that you desire; and to believe it's already yours. Because anything is possible for you. It's happening. It's on its way. It's meant for you.

Action Step

Tap into your imagination. What do you envision for your life? What if the sky were the limit? What would you create, what would you do, who would you be? Take a second now to answer those questions.

If, while doing so, and dreaming about your new normal, you find that your mind is reminding you to be 'realistic,' I invite you to try what Dr. Wayne Dyer suggests and put up a 'Do Not Disturb' sign at the entrance to your imagination. As he says, 'Never, and I mean never, allow anyone else's ideas of who you can and can't become to sully your dream or pollute your imagination.'[11]

CHAPTER 3

Desire

'Small, deliberate actions inspired by your true desires create a life you love."[1]

DANIELLE LAPORTE

In March 2009, my mom and I traveled to Florence, Italy, to visit my sister, who was studying there, and to London. I was excited to get out of Ohio and out of the funk and depression I'd fallen into.

In London, we visited my friend Haley. (She'd moved there to be with a boy she'd met while studying abroad; it was all very glamorous, and I was envious and told her so.)

The moment my mom and I stepped out of Victoria Station, I felt it: the pull. My heart was trying to tell me something. Say what you will, but it felt like magic. It was a feeling I'd experienced during the family trips we took to Chicago (the one other city I'd fallen in love with) at Christmas time, to go shopping. It was like a pull of excitement. I felt it in my body. In my heart.

I felt an element of being at home. Although I didn't act on it that second, or even tell anyone about it, I tucked it in my back pocket and kept it there. It was my little secret, until I was ready to really do something about it a few months later.

During the summer of 2009, I applied for and got a 90-day internship in London. Since Haley had relocated to Paris by that time, I moved in with a friend who knew the city well and stayed until my money ran out (and until he subsequently broke my heart). That period of time in London, more than just a few days, confirmed my suspicions: I was meant to live there. I didn't know why, but I felt the magnetic pull and spent the next few months figuring out how to make it a reality.

Through my research, I discovered that in order to legally live in the city I loved, I either had to marry a Brit or apply for a student visa. Since my British prince was MIA, I went for the latter. However, I wasn't qualified to start a master's degree in psychology, due to the prerequisites being different in the US, so I asked myself what else I wanted to do.

Again, I threw the rulebook out the window. I listened to my heart and heard 'write a book.' So I applied for a spot in a MA program in non-fiction writing and was accepted. I moved to London on August 24, 2010, with four 50-pound suitcases and a dream.

That's what it looks like to be alive to your life and in tune with your desires. You'll start to feel the emotions that come with each opportunity, invitation, trip, visit, introduction – every emotion leaves clues, but the reality is that most people miss them.

Why Desire Matters

As I said earlier, growing up, I remember being taught about personal development, but I don't recall anyone sitting me down and telling me it was okay to follow my heart. I don't remember learning that my heart has the answers. If anything, for most of my life, I've felt ashamed for being so emotional and crying so easily in public places. (More bathrooms than I can count!)

I even remember my high-school boyfriend telling me I'd never be able to help people because I wasn't emotionally stable enough. Emotional and unstable were my understanding of 'heart-centered,' and intuition was just something to use if you found yourself in a dark alley with a suspicious stranger, not something to guide you toward your mission in life.

And I know I'm not alone in this. The reality is that most of us aren't using our heart to its full potential. We forget the resource we have beating in our chest, giving us life and guidance. We listen to everything and everyone outside of ourselves, and wonder why we don't have the life or the results we want.

The Power of Your Heart

Before we go any further, what I want you to really understand is that there's science behind what I'm sharing with you. We're not just talking about your heart having the answers from a spiritual or a metaphysical perspective.

For example, did you know that the heart begins beating in the unborn fetus before the brain even starts to form? And even when it's formed, there's actually much more communication being sent *to* the brain, as there are more fibers leading from the heart to the brain than from the brain to the heart. In fact, nine times more![2]

Yet so many of us are unaware of the heart's power; we're in denial and seemingly oblivious to what we actually want. And the heart is sitting there, beating away, with so much more wisdom (and less ego) than the brain.

So why, you may wonder, are you denying the call of something big? Why are you pretending that you can't hear it and spending so much time in your mind? Again, this isn't your fault. We aren't actually taught to follow our heart as much as we're instructed to 'think' our way to success and the life we want.

We grow up believing that more education or training is the answer. We're instructed to be less emotional, to be masculine, and to keep our head on straight in order to make sensible, respectable decisions. We aren't taught how to use our intuition (I've met people who don't even know they have one). This results in us being so out of alignment with our desires that we're living lives that don't resemble anything we actually want. We're blocking our desires because we aren't tuned in enough to be able to hear them.

- Why do you think so many opportunities pass you by?
- Why do you think you're unaware of what's possible?
- Why do you think you miss your chance?

- Why do you think you're so jealous of everyone you see on social media?

It's because you aren't available to connect with what you truly want, and even when you are, you're not giving yourself permission to actually go for it. Again, you may be asking yourself why that even matters. Well, as author and businessman T. Harv Eker says, 'in order to get what you want, you have to know what you want.'[3] It sounds so simple, yet as I said earlier, so many people are asleep at the wheel of life. They're blind to what's possible and have lost sight of their dreams.

Is that any way to live? Is that a recipe for success? No! You need to know where you're going in order to get there – just as with any cross-country journey, you need a destination. But for many people, comatose has become their default way of living. Let's change that today.

Why We Deny Our Desires

Tell me what you want, and I'll help you get it. Period. Some clients come to me with a laundry list of items – the car, the new house, sending their kids to private school, financial freedom, a book deal. Others haven't thought about it for years – for decades, even. Most of us are barely scratching the surface of our potential and that includes our desires.

During one group coaching session, I asked a client point-blank what she wanted, but she was resistant from the get-go (see how scary dreaming can be for some people!) So, I asked her to simply play a game with me and name one desire. She started with a car – a lightly used Toyota, or something. However, I could tell it was a safe answer, so I asked her again: 'What do you really want?'

After a little more probing, she said: 'A red Mercedes Benz E-Class.' Before I could respond, she quickly interjected with, 'Brand new. So I know no one has farted in it.'

I laughed, but that was exactly what I wanted to hear. I could tell there was something else bubbling beneath the surface. This woman wanted more! She had dreams, and in that moment, she illustrated a reality I see in so many others: the habit of denying dreams. (Note: I use the word 'habit' deliberately here because this truly is habitual; but more importantly, I want you to see that, just like any other habit – biting your nails, snacking, constantly checking Facebook – it's transformable.)

I'm sure you can attest to the fact that we aren't born denying our desires. Just think about your own kids, or babies you're around – they're pretty clear about what they want. And when they start to be able to talk, they're even clearer.

The Fears That Stunt Desire

So why can't we admit what we want? Why do we play it really safe and small and deny the fact that those desires are really ours? In my experience, it all comes down to fear. Here are four reasons why we fall into the habit of denying what we want:

1. **Fear of Disappointment.** It's easier not to think about it. That way you know you won't be disappointed if what you want doesn't happen.

2. **Fear of Judgment.** Maybe you *do* think about what you want from time to time, but you quickly dismiss your goals and declare them crazy or impossible, due to fear of what other people would think.

3. **Fear of Overwhelm.** Maybe you're overwhelmed by the amount of choice, so you get muddled and don't ever make a clear decision about what you want.

4. **Fear of the Desire Itself.** Perhaps your desires are so big that they scare you.

Regardless of which camp you fall into, remember that this isn't your fault! We've been so programmed to stay within the box, to not rock the boat, to not color outside the lines, that we freak out whenever our desires lead us in a direction that isn't the norm. But I want to support you in creating a healthy relationship with desire, starting today.

Acknowledge Your Desires

The first step is for you to start to acknowledge your desires and treat them as if they are real. One of my friends, Love Coach Nicole Moore, believes that our desires are literally 'dropped in' and contribute to the makeup of who we are, like DNA. I love thinking about it like that – just as ideas are real, I believe desires are too. They come from inside us, so how could they not be?

How would things shift for you if you not only acknowledged everything you want but also accepted it as the truth? You'd never question whether your hand is your hand or your heart is your heart, would you? Yet your desires are inside of you and belong to you too. What if you were open to the Universe providing you with everything that you want, based on the simple fact that you want it?

What if you completely owned your desires? How would this transform your life? As writer Genevieve Behrend says: 'Do not fear to be your true self, for everything you want, wants you.'[4]

When you're aligned with your desires, you'll see more momentum in every area of your life.

Think about it – when you truly want something to happen with all your heart, you'll put all your energy and effort toward making it a reality. On the flip side, when something doesn't matter or you're telling yourself you 'should' want it, it will be harder because your heart really isn't in it. (Note: any time 'should' comes into play, you know it's not a true desire!) You won't show up as your best self.

When I'm out of alignment with my heart, progress doesn't happen; my life stalls and I'm only a small fraction of the full person I was created to be. I have less impact, less drive, less energy. That's exactly what happened when I turned the car around – I had no idea what I wanted, but as soon as I opened myself up to listening to my heart (after all, I figured it had got me into this 'mess'!), life became clearer.

Success Tip

Listen to your heart in this moment. What do you want? Whether it's a cup of coffee or making six figures, own it!

Give Yourself Permission

What would it look like if you gave yourself permission to do something small today on behalf of your desires? Maybe you could look for another job, without letting your dad's belief that it would be 'reckless' cloud your desire? Or buy the domain name, without allowing your best friend's voice telling you that it's a 'silly dream' to stop you? What if you went into the designer store, despite the devil on your shoulder (looking a bit like your mother) telling you the place is a rip-off and a waste of money?

I give you permission to do all of the above. And once you start, you'll create your own rulebook and then realize that you don't need any rule besides this: always follow your heart.

By the way, this isn't a one-time thing. You have to continually reevaluate your desires. So many women are living lives they didn't actually want because they miss this crucial step. You're allowed to change your mind and reroute – that's part of giving yourself permission as well.

In her book *Eat, Pray, Love*, Elizabeth Gilbert talks about actively choosing her life – every part of it, from the wedding, to the marriage, to the home – yet it wasn't a forever desire.[5]

So, what's a girl to do? Can you tell if something is a true desire or a fleeting one? Well, it's not as simple as that. Because we're always evolving, you have to start to trust the breadcrumbs scattered along your path of life that are your feelings. You have to trust yourself enough to know when to pivot and when to stay firm to the path. You have to be in tune with your desires and feelings so you're able to tell the difference.

Once more, all you have to do is listen to the whispers. They won't sound like someone whispering in your ear; they'll come to you in the form of an idea, a pull to walk down a certain street, a feeling of jealousy when you're scrolling through Instagram, or a nudge to book a trip. They can even come in the form of unhappiness. Remember, these whispers are like a sound that only a dog can hear: you have to be programmed to be able to receive the message, which starts by you being open. That's it. Then pay attention and wake up to your one life. (Yes, that's an order.)

Remember That You're Worthy

After working with thousands of women around the world, I've seen that worthiness is another key element that we all need to focus on in some form or other. For example, I sent a survey

You don't need any rule besides this: always follow your heart.

containing questions about money to my IHML community because I wanted to get an understanding of how these women view money and making money.

Here are the results, based on the responses we received: 31 percent don't know how to make money; 20 percent are ashamed of their debts; 29 percent have made money and want to make more; 3 percent don't believe there's enough money to go around; and here's the one that hurts my heart: 17 percent don't feel worthy of making a lot of money.

It's one thing to not know how to make money or to be ashamed of debt, but *everyone* is innately worthy of money. However, I see this false belief firsthand nearly every day. For example, whenever my company hosts an event at The Ritz Hotel in London, the feeling of not deserving to be there comes up for most of our clients. They don't think they're far enough along in their business or accomplished enough to be in the luxurious space. Some don't even show up because of that belief. How sad is that?

Trust me, they're not alone in that belief. When I traveled to Australia for the first time, I questioned whether I was worthy of the $7 Toblerone in the mini bar, despite having just spent thousands jetting across the world!

This begs some questions: How much of your life is spent not feeling worthy? How is that holding you back from living your dreams? Or from making the money you desire? How much energy and time are you wasting on the belief? Well, let me tell you the real truth...

- You *are worthy* of the six or even seven figures you're dreaming of.
- You *are worthy* of beautiful clothes for you and your family.
- You *are worthy* of international travel.
- You *are worthy* of organic food.
- You *are worthy* of attending luxury retreats, or events that set your heart and soul on fire.
- You *are worthy* of the work you desire to do in the world.

If someone is out there doing it, you know it's possible for you too. You're already worthy. Whether it's having your own helicopter, traveling First Class, starting your own business, hiring help or moving to your dream country, I want that for you. At least do the research before your rule it out. At least ask the questions. At least get the quote. At least try it once.

Because the thing is, when you block yourself, you also block possibility and opportunity. Remember: your desires are dropped in for a reason – they're meant for you and possible. And that means you're already worthy.

Celebration Break

Let's celebrate all of those statements above. You are worthy of all you desire!

Release Judgment

Whatever we judge, we block. Understanding those five words has transformed my life over the past few years, so I want you to really pay attention to what I'm going to teach you in this section of the book.

First, let me explain why judgment occurs, specifically as it pertains to success. Take the example of wanting to make six figures per year. That's a great goal, but if deep down you're judging all the other six-figure earners, you're going to block yourself from reaching it. Maybe you secretly think they must be greedy or evil; that they tricked or cheated someone in order to make that money; or that it won't last because they'll be reckless with their spending – just like those lottery winners who come into money quickly and then lose it just as fast.

Regardless of the judgment, it's going to come up from beneath the surface and stop you from getting what you want. There's a simple reason why this happens:

If you're judging people who have what you want, your subconscious will stop you from getting it.

This is because, ultimately, you don't want to be judged by yourself! Remember, the ego wants to protect you, so you'll self-sabotage in order to avoid falling into the same category of whoever it is you're judging – even if you outwardly want what they have.

It's just like those middle-school days when you didn't want to fall in with the wrong crowd. If the 'popular kids' were making fun of your best friend, you denied the friendship in order to fit in. It's no different to adults looking to make money and create massive success. We don't want to be judged – and that includes judgment of ourselves. You have to uncover what it is you're judging, because whatever we judge, we block.

Some of these judgments will most likely come out when you're observing and writing down your thoughts. After reading the Mindset chapter, you'll probably naturally start to notice the patterns that come up for you throughout the next few days or weeks. You'll nod when someone points to a beautiful block of houses and says of their owners, 'They're all crooks'; you'll see your friend announcing her promotion on Facebook and wonder if she slept her way to the top; you'll see an Instagram photo of someone posing in a beautiful hotel and judge them for spending their money 'recklessly.'

(And by the way, this pertains to all goals. I once caught myself scrolling through Instagram and judging all the beautiful women with a thigh gap. It was like an out-of-body experience. I heard myself say (in my head): 'How could anyone possibly be that skinny?' Then I realized I was jealous, and I was never going to get in shape – my version of 'in shape' – if I judged women who looked like that.)

Use Your Feelings to Guide You

If you still don't know what you want, start with your feelings. One of the incredible women I've had the pleasure of getting to know in my career is Danielle LaPorte. In her book *The Desire Map*, she says: 'Behind every desire, there is a feeling and your feelings will lead you to your soul.'[6]

So ask yourself, how do you want to feel? Use that to guide you to what you really want. Maybe you want to feel freedom. If so, ask yourself what that would look like. What would bring about that feeling for you? Maybe it's success that you desire to feel. Again, what would bring about that feeling?

Regardless of what it is you want, please stop making yourself wrong, stop judging yourself, stop questioning why your desire exists. Practice owning it instead, and speak to yourself with the same encouragement you'd offer to your best friend. You can truly have anything you want.

Action Step

Create your own list of desires. You can organize them into sections, such as 'Life' and 'Career,' if you like, or do one big list. Also feel free to write them according to your timeline of when you want them to happen. Don't censor yourself – just get everything down on paper.

CHAPTER 4

Purpose

'The world needs that special gift that only you have.'[1]

MARIE FORLEO

As it turned out, my quarter-life crisis decided to follow me across the pond and settle with me in the apartment I moved into after a few weeks of living in a hostel. Whether I was in Ohio or on the other side of the world, the reality was that I still had no clue what I wanted to do with my life.

Around the anniversary of my first year of living in London, my parents came to visit me. It wasn't a planned trip, and I hadn't known I was going to see them, so I hadn't exactly been honest about my current situation. I'd had every intention of painting a rosy picture, but when they stepped into my studio flat, which was the size of a closet, it was obvious, and they knew.

(Oh, and I think the tears during every dinner were a good indication, too. As I said earlier, I've never been able to hide my emotions so I cried

throughout our few days together.) I was 3,000+ miles from home, yet I still wasn't happy, I still didn't know what I was meant for, and I was still broke.

On the last day of the visit, I sat with my dad in front of a church on London's Kensington High Street, mapping out my game plan for my future. Only there wasn't much of a plan. And at that point, my student loan had run out, so I had to ask my dad to lend me $5,000 to get by.

Again, I felt like a failure. I felt like everything was do or die. And I didn't know how to trust my intuition. I made myself wrong for my feelings, instead of accepting them. Of course I have compassion for that version of myself: she didn't know how to tap into that wisdom or get the clarity she was craving.

This confusion and feeling lasted for nearly two more years (and three more apartment moves). I had jobs as a nanny, a personal assistant, and even as a matchmaker, as I tried desperately to find my purpose. But finally, I got the clarity I'd been craving since turning that car around.

In April 2013, while working from home on my laptop for the dating agency, I opened an email from my friend Haley that simply said: 'I thought you'd like this.' Below was a link to a website: www.marieforleo.com. As I explored the content, I immediately felt a huge 'yes!' in my body.

Here was a beautiful woman with great hair, gorgeous clothes, and such a fun brand making a living out of coaching. She was nothing like the coaches I'd encountered in the past: the stuffy men with suits who carried little three-ring binders and went from office to office each day; nothing like the men who'd come to our house to coach my dad when I was little.

And in that moment, I had that feeling again: the one I felt when I arrived in London for the first time and the fear similar to when I turned the car around. This was the second moment my whole life changed course, and in many ways, I felt like I was home. I followed that feeling, and later in 2013, I came up with the idea for I Heart My Life.

The company name came after I realized that I was my ideal client. Everything I'd been through – the evenings spent eating cookie dough and watching The Office *because I was so bored and lonely; the weeks I spent feeling like a failure, or the moments I burst into tears because it wasn't happening fast enough; the times when I was so confused and considered every career option – all of that could be used to help others in a similar place. I had finally found it: my purpose.*

Choice

Purpose. In case it's not obvious, there was a point along my journey when I started to hate that word. And *clarity*. Those two led to the dreaded 'c' word: *choice*. Frankly, all three words have the power to send a modern woman into a frenzy.

At times during my quarter-life crisis (and occasionally today) I longed for a simpler life. It was never about career for my grandma and my mom: they had options, but obviously nothing like what's available today. Sometimes I wondered whether it made it easier for them: that lack of choice.

Of course when it came down to it, I preferred choice over no choice; but I spent so many days feeling overwhelmed by choice, and I knew that so many women felt the same. Maybe we haven't yet learned how to navigate it as a sex, or maybe it's a generational thing – we feel loads of pressure because we want to make the most of our choice. Either way, choice can be painful. Women today are overwhelmed by the choice they have when it comes to 'something big.'

In his book *The Paradox of Choice: Why More is Less*, Barry Schwartz describes my generation as Maximisers: people who have a habit of comparing themselves to others, have a tendency for regret, and a constant fear of failure. For us, Schwartz says, 'The availability of many attractive options means there is no longer any excuse for failure.'[2] For that reason, sometimes, I find myself wondering: what's a girl with choice to do?!

My answer, before I discovered my own intuition and learned to trust it, was to make a list. Growing up, I considered a wide (and I mean really wide!) range of career paths: ER doctor, marine biologist, actress, newscaster, business owner, relationship therapist, wedding planner. I settled on counseling for a while, but then started questioning my choice. When you think you've made a choice and then start to doubt it, you begin to feel like a crazy person. And then the pressure to re-finalize the choice sets in.

During that period when I first arrived in London, I did everything to try to figure it out. But I felt like I had nothing I wanted. Love. Career. Mansion. Kids. Nada. I envied my friends who ended up marrying their high-school sweetheart, becoming teachers, driving Volkswagen Jettas, buying condos, and having kids. It was so simple. Life in a box at 25.

I mean no disrespect by that: as I said, part of me was jealous of the simplicity. Was life meant to be simple? Prescriptive? Then I questioned my own desires: why didn't *I* want that? What was wrong with me? Why was I making really weird decisions compared to the rest of my family? Why did I want so much more? Why did I believe I was meant for more?

Pressure

Here's the thing: life is different now. People aren't the same. We don't get excited about work that doesn't light us up. We want more. As I heard the entrepreneur Noah Kagan state on a podcast at the beginning of my own journey: we are the generation of purpose, not just getting by.[3]

Our generation wants to create a legacy and have an impact. And that's nothing to be ashamed of.

In fact, I believe that now is the best time to be alive and be searching for clarity and following our purpose. But with this quest for purpose added to the mix, there's even more pressure to do something and be great. As you know, I've felt this pressure firsthand, and so have the majority of the women I've worked with.

Get on the Frequency of What You Want

If you're in that place today, I want to support you in getting clearer on the vision you have for your life and the purpose you were put on this planet to fulfill. Even if you already have clarity, you can use what I teach you to go to the next level. We're all constantly reinventing ourselves and nothing we do is permanent. There's always another level and deeper clarity to uncover, and that starts with getting on the frequency of what you desire.

During my quarter-life crisis, what I didn't realize was that I was keeping myself in a perpetual state of confusion. Because I was focused on the fact that things weren't happening for me, and that I lacked clarity, I was emotionally down in the dumps, which meant I was staying stuck and getting more of the same.

If you're thinking about things not working and complaining about them not working, you're going to feel really crappy, and you're not going to take the action required to change your life or attract the opportunities you desire. Make sense?

We're all on a frequency and are attracting opportunities that are also on that frequency, based on how we show up each day. So if you wake up depressed and focused on the fact that you didn't get enough sleep, you're dreading everything on your calendar that day, and hate your life – you're going to get more of that and attract other people who are of the same mindset. There's a reason why misery loves company!

Think about dating or even a marital relationship – you know as well as I do that we're far more attracted to a partner who is positive, confident, and fun to be around; someone who is open to what life has to offer rather than one who's down in the dumps.

If you show up on a date as your worst self, you're going to repel that positive potential partner across from you at the dinner table because you're on different wavelengths. They won't be attracted to you, no matter what you're wearing, how much time you spent on your hair, or the mask of happiness you're trying to display. (And by the way, everything I'm teaching you works with dating too! I believe I was able to attract James – via a cheesy online dating site – in the same way I attracted success, through the tools in this book.)

Celebration Break

Before we go any further, celebrate the fact that you're about to get on the same frequency as your dreams. Do you know how huge that is? Go you!

Become a Magnet to the Life You Want

It's the same with your dreams: you're a magnet in your own life so think about what it is that you're actually attracting right now, based on how you're showing up. This isn't about being perfect – it's about getting on a new, high-vibrational frequency that will attract the life you want instead of repelling it, and lead to the clarity you're craving. Let's take a look at four simple ways to do this:

1. Concentrate on feeling good.
2. Shift your focus.
3. Saturate your mind.
4. Practice gratitude.

1. Concentrate on Feeling Good

The first step is to start paying attention to what makes you feel good. If you're anything like I was in my first year of living in London, you may not be feeling good, but you don't know how to move out of that place. So many of us are slaves to our emotions. We assume we can't shift out of that emotional day, angry moment, or jealous experience. We figure it's just what we have to bear, and that it's the price we pay for being human. That's an exhausting and very defeatist place to be. In the coaching industry, we call it victimhood.

But the truth is, you can take back your power. Our default state is actually meant to be joy. No one is naturally negative – it's a learned behavior just like anything else, and it's not a recipe for success. Feeling good puts you on the frequency of feeling good, and that's where everything you want is.

Feeling good shifts everything and transforms you into the woman you want to be.

In her book *The Fire Starter Sessions*, Danielle LaPorte says, 'Knowing how you actually want to feel is the most potent form of clarity that you can have. Generating those feelings is the most powerfully creative thing you can do with your life.'[4]

So…

What if for one day, you followed what felt good?

What if you then did that for a week or even a year?

How would things shift for you?

I guarantee that *everything* would change.

The best thing you can do for your dreams is follow your bliss – especially in the beginning when you're looking to transform your life or create massive change. So, take a second to think about how you want to feel. Which words come to mind? And then think about what you can do *in this moment* to feel that way.

There's always an answer – even when it feels like nothing's working and it seems impossible, there's always something you can do to feel good. And therefore become the version of you who will attract clarity and opportunity.

2. Shift Your Focus

Another thing I didn't realize during my quarter-life crisis and quest for clarity is that you get what you focus on. By focusing on what's *not working* or on being confused or stuck, we stunt our ability to attract what we *do* want into our lives. Think of it as like riding a bike – when you focus on where you're going, you go there. But when your mind and eyes wander, you start to travel off the path in the direction in which you're looking.

When we're stuck in a personal crisis, period of depression or difficult time in our life, business or career, most of us naturally focus on what's not working. After all, it's right there in front of us, glaringly obvious. But because our mind is focused on the bad, we're unable to see the good. We're also unable to think about the good because our mind can only have one thought at any one time.

It's crucial that you start to train your mind to focus on what's working instead of the opposite. This can be really simple – for example, you could start to make a list every evening of all the things that went right that day (even if it's just two small ones like someone holding a door open for you or receiving a card in the mail). Just like training an unruly puppy, you have to train your mind to start noticing what's working instead of what's not.

3. Saturate Your Mind

One of the ways you can shift your emotional state and frequency is to saturate your mind in as much positivity as possible – so it doesn't have the time or the capacity to be occupied with the negative.

For example, there's a school of thought that when you're trying to lose weight, you shouldn't remove things from your diet – or at least not think about it in that way. Instead, it's better to think about *adding in* healthy food to your diet and as a consequence, you'll be less hungry and forget about the bad food anyway.

Your addiction to junk food will start to subside, and you'll start to crave the good stuff more and more. You'll begin to enjoy new, healthy foods: avocado, green juice, veggie burgers, maybe even kale! You get the idea. It's the same with your thoughts, and we'll look at this in more depth in the next chapter.

4. Practice Gratitude

Around the time of my parents' visit, I started a gratitude practice. I'd been listening to Oprah go on and on about gratitude for decades, so I figured that if I was going to focus on what was currently working, I'd start with that. It seemed simple enough, so every day for a year or so, I wrote out everything I was grateful for in the Tumblr blog I'd created, and posted photos to represent it.

Looking back, it's kind of painful to read it, but I've a lot of compassion for that girl declaring her gratitude for pumpkin spice lattes. Instead of hating the fact that I lived in a tiny studio apartment and loathing my current reality, gratitude enabled me to focus on what was going right – even if it was the coffee I was able to buy and enjoy that day.

There's another thing I want you to know about gratitude, and I think it will be the breath of fresh air you're looking for: you can be in gratitude *and* be driven and desire more, *simultaneously*. So many of us are raised to believe that we just need to be grateful for what we have, and that leaves us thinking that we can't want more.

But that's absolutely not true – I'm grateful every day and I still have plans to take our business to the next level, to build our dream mansion (even though our current home is beautiful), and much more. Drive and gratitude actually go hand in hand and both are essential to creating a life you love.

Engage with Your Life

In addition to getting on the same frequency of what you want, you have to start engaging in your life in order to get the clarity you're craving. Although you may be tempted to check out or allow fate to do its job, please, avoid that temptation. Your dream life is not going to be signed, sealed, and delivered to your doorstep without you showing up. The most important thing is that you start moving in the direction in which your intuition and heart is guiding you. Explore.

Multi-passionate entrepreneur Marie Forleo also advocates this way of thinking, saying that 'Clarity comes from engagement, not thought.'[5] In other words: you'll only be able to tell how you really feel about something when you're engaged with it. See how this is all coming together?

So what *is* engagement? It can be as simple as giving yourself permission to explore your options and ask yourself questions – just like I did when I felt the pull to live in London. Or like Meryl Streep's character (the chef Julia Child) in the movie

Drive and gratitude
go hand in hand
and both are
essential to creating
a life you love.

Julie and Julia, when her husband asks her *what she really loves doing*. Her first response is: 'to eat.'

Success Tip

Ask yourself right now, 'What do I love doing?' And then listen for the answer. Start there. Don't judge, just listen.

Start Engaging Now

I promise, if you do everything I'm about to share, it will lead to your own 'aha' moment and massive clarity.

1. Focus on your strengths.
2. Do your research.
3. Use your jealousy for good.
4. Be selfish (I know you're already freaking out about this one!)
5. Envision your message.

1. Focus on Your Strengths

After working with thousands of women over the past few years, there's one thing I know: we sell ourselves short when it comes to what we're capable of. So when it comes to *your* purpose, focus on where you're at right now and your current strengths. Maybe you're wondering if you have what it takes to go for your dreams. You question whether you're capable and wish you could be further along.

If so, I need you to practice flipping that way of thinking today. Yes, you may need to acquire a new skill, but you'll get there, and I guarantee you already have so much to offer. Start with *where you are now*. For example, if you're starting a business, where are you a step ahead of your ideal client? I guarantee you have knowledge that other people need.

When I started my business, I first helped other women who were in a quarter-life crisis, as I had been. Then, as my business grew, I started to help other entrepreneurs. Where are you a step or two, or five, ahead of your audience?

If you're in a career, what's the next level for you – even if it feels like a leap, where do you want to go? What's the next chapter in your book? There are plenty of things that you are good at right now, in this moment. You have a unique list of experiences that you can use as you move forward. You have your own story – one that literally no one else has. Use it.

2. Do Your Research

You can talk to, or 'interview,' people who are doing what you think you may want to do. For example, before I started my company, I explored different entrepreneurial ventures, one of which was yoga. But as soon as I realized I'd probably need to be qualified to teach yoga – in the event that one of the staff was sick – and that I'd be tied to one location, it was a 'no' for me. It didn't feel right. (Remember, your 'nos' are just as important as your 'yeses.' They help you get clearer as to your feelings.)

Success Tip

Make a list of all the people you'd like to interview or shadow to help you get clearer on your purpose. And if you already know your purpose and are looking to go to the next level or create a new side to your business, this exercise is relevant to you, too!

3. Use Your Jealousy for Good

For most of us, jealousy is a common component of our day-to-day lives. If, while scrolling through Instagram, you see someone you know taking an exciting trip, jealousy rears its head. Or you stumble upon an old boyfriend who somehow managed to get married before you did, and you make it mean something about you. (In case you didn't realize it, jealousy is always about you!)

One of the biggest issues I see today is women not knowing how to handle jealousy. It's another one of those key life lessons that we aren't taught how to navigate. We like to check out and deny our jealousy. We've been taught that it's wrong, and instead of using it to get more clarity about a situation, it stops us. We feel drained because we waste so much energy trying to push it down, and at the same time, it builds up and creates a lack of harmony in the body and detracts from our own power and confidence.

While all this is happening, we're unaware that jealousy can actually give us massive clarity. For example, when you see on a social media post that your old best friend got a raise or started a company and that little feeling rises inside – you know the one I mean: the *why her and not me feeling* – you can use your jealousy for good and as a way to help you get clear on your purpose. All you have to do in that moment is make yourself the observer of your jealousy. Here's how this works…

Imagine taking out your mind from your head, just as you would take off a helmet. Put it in your hand and hold it to the side of your body. Observe it from all angles. Now, while you're observing, make every thought, emotion, and judgment neutral. Not right or wrong, good or evil, just neutral.

If it helps you to think in colors, imagine changing the emotion of jealousy from green to beige. It's just there. It doesn't have a charge – positive or negative – it just is. What is it saying to you? What clarity is it sending your way? Do *you* want a raise, or to make more money? Do *you* want to start that business? In jealous moments, make every emotion the right emotion. Everything you're feeling is a clue.

Everything you're feeling is an indication or sign leading you in the direction of your dream life. Even jealousy.

As Esther and Jerry Hicks say in their book *Money and the Law of Attraction*: 'Any time that you are feeling negative emotion, you are in a very good position to identify what it is that you are, in that moment, wanting – because never are you clearer about what you do want than when you are experiencing what you do not want.'[6]

What does the jealousy mean? What's it telling you? How is it giving you a clue about what you desire in your life? What clarity can you draw from it? How can you turn it from a neutral into a positive? How can you allow it to show you what's possible? How can it be a motivator for you? How can it be the kick in the pants you need to take action?

Celebration Break

You can finally stop beating yourself up for all the jealousy you feel on a daily basis. It's time to use it for good, not evil!

4. Be Selfish

You're selfish. There, I've said it. We're all selfish. We care more about ourselves than anyone else when it comes down to it. In the past, our ancestors had to, in order to survive! Yet for some reason, these days there's a stigma attached to being selfish, and it's gotten a bad rap. I say bring back selfish – in a positive way! You need to have faith in yourself and your ability in order to move forward with your dreams and get the clarity you're craving.

Remember, no one is going to do this for you. No one is going to care as much as you do about your life. And when you think about it, it's not even about being selfish – it's self-*full*. It's the 'full' quality that puts you on the frequency of everything you want. Stop putting yourself and your dreams on the backburner. We get what we focus on, so make your dreams and clarity the focus!

5. Envision Your Message

Here's the final method to help you get clear on your purpose. Ask yourself the following questions:

- If you were to speak on stage tomorrow (or if the *Today* show called you), what would you talk about?
- If you could wake up and share anything with the world, what would it be?
- If you could spend all day every day doing one thing, what would it be?
- What do you feel you were put on this Earth to do? Or be? Or say?

I highly recommend that you try very hard *not* to use your mind as you're answering those questions. Instead, listen to your heart. It has the answers. And remember, you don't have to know the exact path or route. You're allowed to pivot and make changes along the journey, too. Just as Elizabeth Gilbert said in *Eat Pray Love*, you're not getting a tattoo on your face. You can change it. (Okay, she was talking about having kids, but is purpose really that different?)

You need to give yourself a break and remind yourself that nothing is set in stone. You can always scale back or make a change if it doesn't feel right. Think about living your purpose as like that coast-to-coast drive across the US: you can decide to stop off at Mount Rushmore or the Grand Canyon unexpectedly if you'd like. It's just a reroute – people do it all the time!

The most important thing is that you show up. After all, isn't that what purpose actually is? Us showing up for the unique role we were born to play in this one life. This is your time.

Action Step

Ask yourself what shifts you need to make in order to start moving in the direction of your dreams and to get more clarity. Make sure to go through the prompts in this chapter, as they will support you in getting on the frequency of what you desire. Then practice engaging in your life and notice what 'aha' moments you begin to have and what opportunities are attracted to you.

CHAPTER 5

Mindset

'If you want to change the fruits, you will first have to change the roots. If you want to change the visible, you must first change the invisible.'[1]

T. HARV EKER

After discovering coaching, I launched the first version of the I Heart My Life website in March 2014, and just like most driven women (in particular new entrepreneurs), I thought everything would happen quickly. Although I didn't expect a sudden influx of customers, I hadn't realized it would take months to make a penny. In fact, it took until July 2014 for me to make any money, and even then, it was only $442 that came in during a call I took on a park bench while on a family trip to Sausalito, California (which my parents paid for).

The months that followed weren't easy. In fact, I went through a period of 54 'nos' in a row from people who didn't want to work with me. Call after call, I heard, 'This sounds great, but I don't have the money.' Or 'I need to ask my husband.' And the elusive, 'I'd love to, but I have to plan my daughter's birthday party.' (Really?!)

During that time, I battled thoughts like, Who am I to do this? Does Marie Forleo already have all the clients in the world? Her hair is better than mine. I'm not good on video. What in the world would I even talk about? I've never run a business. I suck with money. I have no money. I'm broke. *Mind chatter like that is a total dream killer, and it will stop you in your tracks if you let it, as it almost did for me.*

During the fall of 2014, I remember getting on a call with one of my coaches. The night before, I'd filled out her pre-call form and let her know which things 'weren't working,' and to the questions 'What are you most proud of' and 'What are you most excited about,' I'd answered 'nothing.'

On our call, my coach told me that I was like a pot on the stove about to boil. I was heating up and about to see the bubbles, but I had to start to transform my mindset and focus on what I wanted to happen, not on what I didn't. Luckily, I chose to listen to her.

Looking back, I'm so grateful for those 54 nos because they resulted in me immersing myself in transforming my mindset, which snowballed into me falling in love with mindset work to the extent that it's truly my mastery today. The internal shifts also resulted in external ones. For example, I celebrated my first $6,000 month, which meant I was able to leave my 9–5 job and run I Heart My Life full-time. That's the power of mindset.

And yet, most people don't realize that success is actually an inside job. In his book *Leveraging the Universe*, Mike Dooley says that 'your thoughts, words and actions create your reality.'[2] I also love how T. Harv Eker describes this and what he calls the Process of Manifestation in his book *Secrets of the Millionaire Mind*. He says that 'Thoughts lead to feelings. Feelings lead to actions. Actions lead to results.'[3]

We covered this topic briefly in Chapter 4, but this chapter is about you fully integrating it and understanding what it actually means for you and your success. Get ready for *everything* to change today. (Yes, literally.) It did for me, and it will for you too.

Your Mind Today

In his *The Successful Mind Podcast*, bestselling author David Neagle explains that the role of the subconscious mind is to keep us safe: 'It's not programmed to make more money, start a business – it was at one point, but along the way, the harmful programming took over: like a virus that stops it from functioning properly.'[4]

Launching a website, moving to another country, asking for a raise, or increasing your prices, none of these are moves the mind deems 'safe' so it will tell you it's impossible, that you can't do it, that you're a fraud, that you're not good enough – anything it can think of to get you to stop. It will pull out and deliver from your mental library examples of things that didn't work out in the past, just to prove it to you; or it will teleport you into the future and pretend to have powers of prediction that convince you there's no possible way you'll actually reach your goal.

Essentially, your mind is full of rulebooks created over the span of your lifetime (we've talked about a few of them in previous chapters) – written and installed when you were a child and based on society's and your parents' viewpoints, all passed down from generation to generation. You learn through what you were told, what you experienced, and what you observed.[5]

We bring those rulebooks into adulthood and believe (naively) that we have everything we need to achieve our dreams. However, we soon realize that we're operating with faulty, very outdated rules that are not in service to our success. Little do we know that we've actually been programmed to stay safe! (For the purposes of this book, that doesn't mean *physically* safe, which is different. When you read 'safe' replace it with 'stuck'.)

The truth is: you need a mindset makeover to reach your goals.

You have to *become* the woman who reaches those goals. You have to *become* the person who's able to achieve what she wants to achieve. Just like an athlete who trains for the Olympics and visualizes the results they want, you too need to create new habits, and that starts in your mind.

The Truth about This Work

Before we go any further, you should know that there's a bit of bad news – if you choose to look at it that way – about this work we're doing. The reality is that it's never really done; but it does get way easier.

When I was starting my business, I had to do a lot of work to shift the natural Negative Nancy that was my mind. It was as if my compass was set toward what *wasn't* working – that I wasn't good enough or skinny enough, and so on – and that there was something wrong with me and my current reality.

In order to shift out of that habit of thinking, I spent hours every day repeating certain phrases, listening to audios in the shower, and reading about how to transform my mind in order to change my current reality – which you'll learn more about in this chapter. Today, although I still feel fear and lack confidence from time to time, my 'bounce back' is quicker. Think of it as like a rubber band snapping back into place: the bigger the rubber band, the longer it takes to bounce back. James and I like to call this our 'bounce back-ability.'

This work is about you shifting your mindset in a way that makes the rubber band much smaller and tighter, so the bounce back is much quicker, almost instantaneous. Your range of emotions will be much smaller, too, as you'll stay in that positive frequency much more often. Just as if you were training for a race or a marathon, you'll still get out of breath but you'll recover more quickly and you'll extend your limits; so you're no longer stopping at 40 percent but 50 percent, then 60 percent and so on. This is what we're creating right now, together.

The good news is that once you do this initial overhaul and dive deep into this work, you'll have created your own backup generator that's ready to kick in when you need it. Now, I'm not saying there won't be days or even weeks when you'll feel emotions like sadness and stress – you're human, not a robot – but this work will free you from the control your mind has over you at the moment.

Right now, you're not the one running the show. You're a slave to your mind, and that's not going to get you the life you want. That changes starting today, and although you'll have to continue this work forever, especially when you reach new levels of success, everything will feel easier after this initial step.

Thought Habits 101

Put simply: your mind is not your friend. As you've already learned, it wants to keep you safe and small and it doesn't understand change or the desire to do something new and different. We're going to go much deeper into this subject in this chapter, so you have an even greater understanding of how the mind works when it comes to your success and your dreams, and how to transform your old programming.

You should also know that your brain is lazy, and it likes to optimize itself as much as possible. So when recurring thoughts become a 'habit' it decides to make those thoughts automatic. This means it no longer has to reassess every situation from scratch – instead, it will just pull up what you usually think about a given situation, person, or opportunity.

For example, if as a teenager you were left feeling betrayed in some of your relationships and uncertain about who you could trust, today you may hesitate at the thought of letting anyone in. Or maybe your parents taught you that spending too much money is bad – that you should only spend the minimum and just be happy with what you have. So as you grow up you never strive for more than is necessary to survive, and you fail to truly satisfy your desires and ambitions around what is possible for you.

We have more thoughts per day than we can even quantify; some research says 15,000 and others, 90,000 – regardless, it's a lot, and most of them are the same ones we've been having for years. They're on repeat and they aren't serving us. These are thoughts such as:

- I'm not good enough.
- It's not possible.
- It's not going to work out.
- Who am I to do this?

The good news is that we can actually take back our power over the mind. Just like other habits in our lives – working out (or not working out), biting our nails, leaving the butter out on the kitchen counter – we have habitual ways of thinking, 'thought habits,' that are stopping us from getting the results we want. But there are ways in which we can hack that system and create a new playlist.

Our Addiction to Negative Thinking

One more thing – you may be asking yourself why anyone would continue to think in a way that's harming them, keeping them from their dreams, stopping them from making money or having an impact. Maybe you're wondering why it's so difficult to break free from your own thought habits. After all, you don't *want* to be thinking that way.

The truth is that we're addicted to negative thinking, and because we're addicted and the programming is so deep, it's going to take time to break those habits. And your mind will fight you every step of the way. Just as it is with any habit, you're actually getting something from it. For example, maybe these thought habits are enabling you to stay safe. You're allowed to not ask for the raise, take the trip, start the business, because your mind told you it wasn't possible – it's your own Get Out of Your Dreams for Free card!

Your mind is comfortable with where you are today, and comfort is its #1 priority. It's like the woman who stays with the man who abuses her because she grew up with abuse – it's horribly sad, but familiar. All that changes today. Your mind doesn't get to run the show any longer – at least not in this same way.

Two Different Mindsets

In her classic book *Mindset: The New Psychology of Success,* Stanford University psychologist Dr. Carol Dweck coined two terms to describe the underlying beliefs, or mindsets, people have about learning, talent, and intelligence.[6]

- **The fixed mindset.** People with this believe they only have a certain amount of talent and intelligence, and that such qualities are fixed. (In other words, just be happy with what you've got because this is as good as it's going to get!)

- **The growth mindset.** In this, people believe their basic qualities can be developed through their efforts. Everyone can change and grow with experience. (In other words, anything is possible and always changing.)

I'm sure you can guess which type of mindset creates the success you're after – the growth mindset. The good news is that you were born with a growth mindset. For example, most of us grew up dreaming and believing in the impossible – we were little girls without limits. We dreamt of being a princess, an astronaut, or a doctor. But then at some point, the word 'realistic' became a part of our vocabulary and everything started to change.

We no longer focused on growth and what was possible, and instead, became obsessed with limits and the reasons why we *couldn't* do something. The good news is that your inner child is still there, and you can access her to achieve more success. It's time to reunite yourself with your dreams and desires.

Money Mindset

Although I could (and will) write an entire book about money mindset, this chapter isn't about this topic in particular. However, as it's a key part of mindset we'll look at it briefly. The truth is that most people don't realize they have habitual ways of thinking about money too.

Your money mindset is made up of the beliefs about money that are passed down through generations and develop through what you learn about money. Some common money stories are as follows:

- 'Making money is hard.'
- 'There's never enough money.'
- 'Money doesn't grow on trees.'
- 'Rich people are evil.'
- 'Don't be selfish.'
- 'Talking about money is icky.'

As you can see, these ways of thinking aren't going to get you closer to the life you desire (if financial freedom is part of that dream life). (And if you're wondering whether this applies to you, just take a look at your bank account today: your current financial reality will give you an idea of your past thinking.[7] So if you don't like the number staring back at you, it's time to take a look beneath the surface.)

If financial transformation is what you're after, use the tools and information I'm going to share with you to create those financial shifts in your life.

Observe the Quality of Your Thoughts

Whenever we're looking to reach a big goal – for example, run a marathon – most of us realize that we have to be acutely aware of certain things, such as what we're putting in our body, how much exercise we get, what our schedule looks like, how much sleep we get. But many don't realize that we also have to be acutely aware of what we're *thinking*.

It's the same with starting a business, losing 20 pounds, or making six figures. Yet so many of us are unaware of that truth. We aren't taught to pay attention to our thoughts. But as Robin Sharma says, 'you don't have the luxury of even one negative thought,'[8] when your desire is complete life transformation.

Once again, you can think about your mind as an operating system that was developed during your childhood, and when you bring it into adulthood, it most likely doesn't serve you anymore. It doesn't allow you to reach your goals. It stops you from moving forward. Your mind needs an updated system to function accordingly – especially if you're looking to hit big goals and change your life. So, how do you know what operating system you're actually using, so you can hurry and update it?

At a yoga class I attended years ago, the instructor said something I absolutely loved: pay attention to the 'quality of your thoughts.' I'd never heard it put quite like that before. Are you experiencing the thoughts of someone who's just getting by? Maybe the same ones you had throughout a personal crisis in the past? Or are they millionaire-level, high-quality thoughts? Success starts with your mindset, so the quality of your thoughts needs to be super high caliber to get the results you want. That's how people get to the top.

In order to truly understand what's going on in your mind, and the ways in which you may be sabotaging your success, you have to start tracking the thoughts you're thinking about things outside of you and yourself.

To understand your mind you must become an observer and an avid note-taker of your thoughts.

Any time you start to feel anxious, sad, or lacking in confidence, *write down the thought* from which that feeling stems. Remember when we talked about taking out your mind, like you'd remove a helmet from your head? My suggestion is to start to observe your mind and make every thought, emotion, and judgment neutral. Get curious instead of judgmental about those thoughts that are coming in, moment by moment. This has to become part of your daily practice for you to be able to take back control of your life.

Success Tip

Try this exercise, which I ask my clients to do in the very beginning of our time together. Observe your thoughts for at least 48 hours, and write them down, using a note-taking app on your phone, such as Evernote. Pay particular attention to any sort of powerful emotion that comes up (be that *positive or negative*, as both give us positive insight).

Whenever you want to reach a big goal, you have to be acutely aware of what you're thinking.

In those moments when you feel unstoppable, on top of the world, what are you thinking? And conversely, in those moments when you fall into complete despair and are unable to get out of bed, let alone move forward with your dreams, what are the specific thoughts that are holding you back?

This also pertains to the thoughts we think about our capabilities. As women, we're often so self-critical, and say things to ourselves that we'd never dream of saying to a best friend – and those are the words we're using to create our reality! The real truth is that treating yourself in a way that you'd never treat someone else is no recipe for success. You may think that tough love is the way to get results, but in my experience, that's not the case.

Of course hard work is necessary to reach most big goals, but it's actually counterproductive for you not to be kind to yourself during the process. If you want to be one of the world's most successful people, it's essential that you transform the way you treat yourself. We'll cover this topic more in the Self chapter. If you're anything like me (and my clients!), what you'll discover about your language and thoughts will be pretty shocking, but don't worry, there's a way to change this way of thinking.

Upper Limits

One of the most inspirational books I read at the beginning of my own journey to something big was *The Big Leap* by Gay Hendricks. A psychologist and teacher, Hendricks is known for his work on a concept called the 'upper limit.' An upper limit is a glass ceiling of sorts that stops us from reaching what he calls our Zone of Genius.

He says, 'Each of us has an inner thermostat setting that determines how much love, success, and creativity we allow ourselves to enjoy. When we exceed our inner thermostat setting, we will often do something to sabotage ourselves, causing us to drop back into the old, familiar zone where we feel secure.'[9]

Once you're clear on your own thought habits and the reason why you may be stuck in patterns that aren't serving you, you can start to also pay attention to the upper limits that are stopping you from reaching your goals and dreams.

For example, in my coaching work, I often find that my clients have an upper limit on the amount of money they can make, and it's based on what their family or society told them was possible for them at an early age. My goal is to support them in seeing that six figures or seven figures (and beyond) is possible for them, and there for the taking. It's time for you to do the same and bust through your own upper limits.

Transforming Your Mindset

As you can imagine, shifting your negative thoughts and upper limits takes time, attention, and practice – after all, you've been engaged in habitual thinking for decades. But I'm going to give you some simple ways to see a huge transformation, starting today.

My advice is to take note of what resonates with you in the rest of this chapter. You're welcome to pick and choose a few action steps to try first, and then come back to this part of the book later on, to give the rest of them a go. Either way, you have to *immerse* yourself in this work and new way of thinking. It can't be something you dabble in. In case you didn't know, dabblers don't get results. Well, they do, but tiny, dabbling ones, and you're better than that. It's important to make this non-negotiable.

Ways to Shift Your Mindset

Let's now look at four ways you can start to make the transformation:

1. Saturate your mind (again).
2. Flip the switch.
3. Use Post-It notes and screensavers.
4. Choose your words carefully.

1. Saturate Your Mind (again)

In an interview conducted before she passed away, Louise Hay spoke about the way people delusionally (my word, not hers) believe they're going to create change or the life they want by practicing positive thinking for a small percentage of the day while spending the rest of the time in self-pity, negative thinking, despair, or victim mentality. But that's not how this works.

Let me give you an example. There was a point in my life when I lost 25 pounds (11kg) by not working out. Yes, you read that correctly. For years, I struggled with weight gain, especially as I was building my business. There were periods when I worked out six times a week – spinning, yoga, running – but nothing seemed to change.

Finally, I went on a plan that reset my metabolism and helped me completely change my diet. It may seem obvious, but I started to see that what I put into my body was the key to weight loss, not the exercise. So now I try to eat in this new way for 90 percent of the time throughout the week. Obviously, sticking to the plan 100 percent of the time would elicit even more results – but I'm not available for a life without pizza.

It's the same for your mind; as we discussed in the Purpose chapter, one of the ways you can shift your emotional state is to saturate your mind in as much positivity as possible. Is your mind in the gutter for a majority of the time? Are you thinking it's not possible to reach your goals, or that you're not worthy and deserving?

It's important to observe every aspect of your day: from your initial morning thoughts when the cortisol in your body is higher, to midday lunch thoughts when you feel tired, to what you're thinking in the evening before bed. What's the pattern of the playlist that's going through your mind, and is it serving you? If not, what can you do to make it a more positive one?

Another thing I recommend is paying attention to what you're allowing into your mind. For example, the TV shows or movies you watch on a regular basis. Since doing this work, I've become highly sensitive to what's on TV and the movies I watch. There's so much happening in the world that can leave us feeling depressed, so in my downtime, I prefer watching things that light me up and end with everything working out, tied neatly in a bow. Like the Hallmark Channel movies I'm obsessed with during Christmas time or comical clips of the Ellen DeGeneres Show. I want to watch things that make me feel good. (Remember how important feeling good is?)

It's the same with your thoughts – what program is your mind tuned in to? What are you feeding it? Remember: this is all about you saturating your mind and keeping it on a short leash so it doesn't stray. You have to use language that reflects what it is you want to achieve.

2. Flip the Switch

Once you have a list of all the harmful thoughts that are going through your mind, or at least an understanding of them, you can saturate your mind with a new way of thinking by using a technique called 'flipping the switch.' (I didn't coin this term but I can't recall where I first heard it.)

Flipping the switch is simple, but it takes practice and focus. It works like this: whenever those negative thought habits creep up, you can start to flip them to the opposite thought. Here are some examples:

- I suck at making money. → Money flows effortlessly to me.

- I can't run my own business. → I'm running a successful business now.
- I'll never write a bestselling book. → I'm a *New York Times* bestselling author.

This process is all about retraining your mind to create new thought habits. Again, the easiest way to think about it is to imagine you're creating a new playlist that's going to support you in reaching your dreams. (We all know there are certain songs that make us run faster at the gym!)

Please know that in the beginning, it can feel like you're lying to yourself, or as if what you're saying isn't actually real. That's okay – start with what feels good to you. Maybe that means something smaller, and building up from there. Just keep moving forward with flipping the switch. Soon enough, it will start to feel like second nature and the truth – just like any other new habit you create. (We all know that green juice didn't taste good at first!)

That new playlist will help you get the results you want – like listening to your favorite song while running on the treadmill (versus that meditation music that puts you to sleep). There's power in the playlist.

3. Use Post-It Notes and Screensavers

Once you've retrained your mind and created new, flipped phrases to focus on – 'I'm worthy of everything I want' versus

'I'm not worthy' – put up Post-It notes around your house displaying this new way of thinking. When I was first retraining my mind during that period of 54 nos in a row, I had these notes all around the house – on the refrigerator, the bathroom mirror, the front door. Now I have them stuck to my desktop computer. Choose a place that works for you: somewhere you're guaranteed to see the phrases throughout the day.

You can also create screensavers for your computer or phone that display your new phrases. Even if you're not a designer, there's plenty of software out there that will allow you to make a quick graphic, or you may even be able to find your phrases on Pinterest. (One of my colleagues actually had her financial money goals made into a T-shirt. Bonus points if you take it to that level!)

4. Choose Your Words Carefully

Cancel, clear, delete. No, I'm not asking you to reset your computer: I'm showing you how to reset your mind. As you're creating new programming, it's essential that you choose your words like you choose your clothes. Be more deliberate in your life. Don't speak just to speak. Speak your dreams into reality and remember that your thoughts, words, and actions create that reality.

Don't worry – it's okay if you forget from time to time, or if a 'I suck at this' or 'It's never going to work' come out. Just say 'cancel, clear, delete' and bring yourself back to the present and what you want to happen. Let me give you an example:

Speak your dreams into reality, and remember that your thoughts, words, and actions create that reality.

more recently than I care to admit, I shared with James that one of my current fears is that I'm not going to reach the level of success I desire because I'm an introvert and don't actually like spending time with big groups of people, networking and socializing.

The moment those words came out of my mouth, I knew it was a 'cancel, clear, delete' moment. I didn't want to put that out into my reality. I believe that I create my reality, and I'd already decided that I'm going to be a wildly successful introvert. There are plenty of them out there! Why not me? (If you identify with being an introvert and wonder how that may affect your success, we'll be covering this topic later in the book.)

No Room For Self-Doubt

Also look out for your use of hesitant or uncertain words. Here's an example – in our coaching programs, every time we start a new group or cohort, we invite our clients to a 'Welcome to the Program' phone call. During these, I ask each person to introduce herself and share her goals. And let me tell you, these women know how to dream big! Here are a few common themes...

- Have a five-figure month by the end of the program.
- Launch my website and get visible to all my friends and family.
- Gain independence by making more money and moving into my own place.

- Be able to quit my 9–5 and run my business full-time.
- Move to my dream city.
- Create a business that allows me the freedom to spend more time with my kids.
- Revamp my current business so it's aligned with my true passion.
- Start making big money for myself (rather than for someone else).
- Take my dream trip.

However, as my clients describe their intentions and dreams, there's usually one word that comes up: *hopefully*. I'm sure this is a word you use throughout your day and week as well. Maybe to you it's not a big deal, but let me share a dictionary definition of it with you: *All being well; it is to be hoped that; if all goes well; if everything turns out all right; God willing; most likely; with luck; probably; conceivably; feasibly.*[10]

Seems a bit wishy-washy, right? Would you bet your life on *hopefully*? No! In fact, I feel so strongly about this that I've eliminated the word from my vocabulary. When we qualify, or restrict, our goals and dreams by using words such as hopefully, we're communicating doubt; the word hints at the fact that we don't 100 percent believe that they are possible, and who wants that?

For instance, 'I'm hopefully going to start working with clients this month' doesn't have the same power as 'I'm going to start working with clients this month.' Or 'I'm hoping to get a raise in the next quarter' versus 'I'm getting a raise in the next quarter.' The former communicates doubt, while the latter tells the Universe that this goal is non-negotiable for you – that it's going to happen, one way or another.

And if there's one thing I've learned when it comes to mindset and dreams, it's that there's no room for self-doubt. You have to believe in yourself and your dreams full force. You have to really, truly trust that your dreams are possible for you in order to see the success you want.

Doubt kills dreams. It's up to you to fortify your mindset so it can reject doubt.

Again, your thoughts and words create your reality – and if you're thinking and communicating in a way that doesn't make your goals non-negotiable, then your reality isn't going to reflect what you truly desire. Your mind actually doesn't know the difference between what *has* happened and what hasn't *yet* happened. That's why this is so key. It also doesn't know the difference between 'I won't fail' and 'I will fail' – because in both phrases, the focus is on failure. Flip it to 'I will succeed' instead.

Your choice of words should make you feel good, too. For example, when I first started doing this work, I also eradicated the words 'expensive' and 'debt' from my vocabulary because they made me feel limited and anxious. (I changed expensive to 'premium' and debt to 'investments'.)

You, too, need to start recognizing your own patterns in language and what feels good and what doesn't. This is about communicating to the Universe, God, yourself – whatever you believe in – that what you desire is possible, and that it's already on its way to you. There's simply no room for 'hopefully,' 'maybe,' or 'someday' when it comes to your dreams.

Visualizing

You may have been visualizing without knowing it for years. For example, I saw a quote graphic on Instagram with an image of Alicia Silverstone as Cher in the movie *Clueless* in class, holding up her pink feather pen. It said 'I used to get in trouble for daydreaming at school. Little did they know that I was VISUALIZING.' Visualizing is daydreaming with massive intention behind it. It could also be considered meditation or prayer. It's simple to do and a hugely underused tool we have at our disposal.

In 2014 I used visualization to get an upgrade on a flight to the US for a conference with my coach. Every day in the run-up to my trip, I sat silently and pictured myself walking onto an airplane and, instead of making my way to the back and the economy seats, I saw myself touching the beautiful leather Business Class seats. I saw myself putting my carry-on bag safely above my head, and not having to fight for space in the overhead locker, sitting down in my comfy seat, and immediately being handed a glass of champagne; I then stretched my legs, only to discover I had more room than I needed.

An hour later, I saw myself being handed a gorgeous plate of food on a tablecloth, and silverware instead of plastic utensils – it was like eating in a five-star restaurant in the air. And most importantly, I felt the feelings associated with having that reality. And it worked! I was upgraded to Premium Economy on Virgin Airlines (their version of Business Class). I couldn't believe it!

Take a Lesson from Top Athletes

One study has even shown that athletes who visualize and practice the results they want are much more likely to reach them than those who just practice.[11] Isn't that incredible?

One of my favorite examples of the power of visualization is Amy Purdy, an Olympic snowboarder who was diagnosed with meningitis in her early 20s and had to have her legs amputated to save her life. I first heard her speak when I went to Oprah's 'Live Your Best Life' event, where she shared her powerful story with us.

When Amy discovered what the doctors had to do in order to save her life, she made the decision that she was still going to do what she'd always intended, despite the loss of her legs. So she set her mind on her dreams, not on what was about to change for her physically. She visualized herself skiing down the mountain. She felt the wind blowing through her hair, the icy air on her face, and the heavy Olympic medal being placed around her neck and against her chest.

A few years later, not only did she win that medal, but she also went on to dance on *Dancing with the Stars*, speak on stage in front of thousands of people, write a book, and start a business that creates shoes for women with prosthetic legs.

Visualization has everything to do with feeling and getting on the same frequency of what you want.

We hear stories like these all the time, but rarely do we take the time to try visualization ourselves or really understand it. Visualization works because when you tell the mind you've done something, it doesn't know if it's happening now or in the future. As I said earlier, it can't tell the difference. And when you expect that something is on its way, you're more likely to take the action in support of that belief. For example, Amy kept training, she kept focusing on her medal, she showed up – and she got the result she'd envisioned.

So, get yourself to the place where you can feel yourself…

- Celebrating a six-figure income.
- Getting a thank-you email from your dream client.
- Taking the trip abroad.

- Feeling beautiful during your first photoshoot.
- Filling your group program.
- Being interviewed on your favorite talk show.

And remember, your mind is a magnet and everything you want wants you back. Expect it to be on its way.

Celebration Break

Before we dive into the next topic, I want you to celebrate all the work you've done so far – you've learned about thought habits, have an understanding of how the mind works, and how it's holding you back, and you've started to reprogram it so that it gets you the success you want. This is going to be a game-changer for you. Cheers to you!

Understanding Fear and Worry

Even after all that work to transform your mindset, you may find that fear and worry about your future still creep into your thoughts. And please know that in those moments, you're definitely not alone.

In her book *Big Magic: Creative Living Beyond Fear*, Elizabeth Gilbert bluntly declares that her 'fear is boring.'[12] Is your fear boring, too? Has it been playing the same song, over and over again? Has it stopped you from moving forward with your dreams and creating a life you really love? So why are you continuing to give it so much power? Think about it like this: if you're allowing the fear to take over, or you're playing the victim who isn't capable or doesn't have a choice, do you think you're actually going to move forward with your dreams and hit your goals?

No. At least not without shifting something internally. And remember, you can only have one thought at any given time, so it's up to you to choose one that's actually going to serve you (and we both know that's not fear!)

In *The Big Leap*, Gay Hendricks describes fear as merely 'excitement without breath.'[13] I bet you never thought about it that way. Think about how you feel before getting on a rollercoaster. Excited *and* scared, right? What if you allowed your fear to actually be a sign of excitement instead of the big STOP sign it is right now? How much would your life change? How much more success would you be able to create? How would that decrease your level of anxiety?

What Worry Really Is

At the beginning of building my business, I worried about what people would think (keep reading to see how to handle that one!); how I'd make money; if anyone would actually buy what I was selling; how I'd get to where I wanted to go. This is normal, and I'd imagine you've had similar worries. In fact, most of us are addicted to worry.

When we go deep into the subconscious mind, we learn that worry stems from what our parents taught us, or from a specific past experience. As you were growing up, you probably did have something to worry about; but now, your reality isn't the same, yet you're still worrying. Remember, the mind will pull from the 'previous experiences library' to predict the future. It wants you to stay safe (stuck) so it brings up these worries based on past experiences in the hope of deterring you from moving forward. But this doesn't have to be your forever reality. You can be free from worry.

Worry = A Nail in Your Tire

I'm proud to say that, after decades of being a chronic worrier, I've made my peace with worry. In fact, there was one moment fairly recently when I woke up and realized that I was done. Something shifted in me, and I started to think about the actual ROI (return on investment) of my worry. I couldn't come up with one. single. thing. In fact, my worry has caused me nothing but stress, backaches, sleepless nights, fights with James – literally nothing positive.

In fact, worry is like a nail in a tire, and *you* are the tire. It starts as a small hole that gets bigger and bigger over time. More and more worries results in more and more holes, and eventually you're left with a flat, non-functioning tire. You literally become deflated because worry sucks your energy.

And the reality is that changing your life and achieving your dreams takes a lot of effort; you need all the energy you have in order to make your dreams a reality. You can also think about yourself as a bucket filled with water. You have a certain amount of water (energy) available to you, and when you worry, it uses up your energy and you no longer have access to as much as you did before the worry came into play. See, no ROI. And the sad (but also exciting) truth is that most of our worries never actually happen. Yet we still expend so much energy on them. Think about what you could create/do/achieve with that energy instead!

Replace Worry and Fear with Action

Here's a simple way to move past fear and worry: take action even though it's there. Trust me, fear is with me every step of the way, but it no longer gets to run the show. As Elizabeth Gilbert says, fear can be in the car but it doesn't get to touch the radio and it definitely doesn't get to drive.[14] Taking action is how you kick fear out of the driver's seat. After all, there can only be one driver.

So, decide that today's the day you're going to take action, despite the fear. Decide that you're not going to let the 'what ifs' or the 'what if it doesn't work outs' run the show. I've a whole chapter on Action coming up in the book, so stay tuned.

A Final Note

At this point in the book, I feel like it's my job to tell you that you are extraordinary. What you've just uncovered in this chapter alone is not only essential to your success but also work that most people don't do in their entire lifetime. Take time to celebrate the changes you've already created in your life and those that are about to become more apparent over the passing days. You're incredible.

Action Step

Once you have a list of your harmful thoughts, choose at least one negative belief and practice replacing it with a new more positive thought and visualize what you desire. Observe that changes that happen in your life due to this powerful step.

CHAPTER 6

Goals

'Your ability to discipline yourself to set clear goals, and then work toward them every day, will do more to guarantee your success than any other factor.'[1]

BRIAN TRACY

After leaving my 9–5 job in October 2014, and going full-time in my business, I started to really see what was possible for me financially, and my goal was simple: hit six figures by my 30th birthday (a year later).

The funny thing about goals is that often times, people pull them out of thin air. I was no different. Six figures had always been the goal for me. (I wanted seven figures but I assumed that would come at some point in my 40s.) To me, six figures meant that I'd really made it. I was doing something legit.

The only problem was that I had no idea how to get there. But luckily I saw other people out there doing it in my industry, so I knew it was possible. (See how important possibility mindset is!) For example, I distinctly remember my coach telling me that I could turn my yearly salary as a matchmaker into my monthly revenue. I wasn't sure how that was going to happen, but I loved the sound of it, so I chose to believe her. (Those mirror neurons were firing!)

My coach helped me decide on the goal of signing up 10 clients for my one-on-one coaching program in November 2014. She let me know that it was all I was to talk, think, or write about until all 10 spots were gone. I followed her orders, and it worked!

I celebrated my first five-figure month that November – over $19,000. Before the end of 2014, I'd registered 25 clients in a group program as well. And by January 2015, I'd hit six figures in my business – six months after registering my first client and 10 months before my 30th birthday.

Goal-Setting 101

As someone clearly very wise once said, 'If you don't have a plan, you plan to fail.' Often times, the hardest thing for entrepreneurs and driven people is knowing what they really want. Plus, so many of us are multi-passionate. We want to do *all* the things.

Trust, me, I'm no different, but another key factor in maintaining momentum in my first year of business was learning to focus on and set achievable goals – as well as take massive action until I saw the results I wanted. Just like an athlete looking to get a medal or break a record, I had to be focused on what I wanted and not lose sight of it until it was mine. And I had to take the *right* action.

Think about it like this – if you're looking to gain 10 pounds, the action you'll take is very different to that you'll take if you're looking to lose 10 pounds. And although most people claim they know which goal they're working toward, in my experience they don't actually know how to goal-set in a way that primes them for success and facilitates consistent effort. We'll cover both issues in this chapter.

I'm going to break this process down for you even more now, so you can really understand how it works, see the importance of it, and learn how to apply it to your own life to see the success you want. However, as always, I need you to first recognize what's possible, not just for me, but for you too.

And by the way, in this chapter, I'm focusing heavily on financial goals and milestones – because as a business owner, that's what I tend to goal-set around. But if your goals aren't specifically money-related, that's okay. Use the information and examples I give you and apply them to your goal.

2D Goals

Before we go any further, I need you to understand that your goals are two-dimensional – you have your big-picture goals, but you also have your short-term goals: the ones that lead you to the big-picture vision. As a driven woman, you have to learn how to focus on both types of goal *simultaneously*. This means thinking about the big-picture goal – let's say a trip to California – as well as the current reality, which in this case is navigating the traffic as you leave New York City. It's a dance to keep both places in mind.

The first step is to actually get clear on your big-picture goals. What is it that you want to achieve? Is it starting a business? Buying your dream house? Moving up the ladder in your career? Getting into the best shape of your life? Being a guest on *Super Soul Sunday*? Landing in *Forbes*? *You* get to decide. (I hope you know this by now!)

If your goals are still a bit foggy, revisit the list of desires you wrote earlier (in Chapter 3). Maybe your desires have changed or morphed since then – remember, you're allowed to adjust them: they're yours!

Once you have the big picture in mind, you have to ask yourself what this journey is about for you. Which steps toward the big-picture goal do you feel called to take right now? Maybe you want to hire someone to help you map that out, like I did, and take the guesswork out of it. Or maybe you have a strong intuition about where you need to start. Regardless, starting requires you to also be clear on your short-term goals. Otherwise, you'll end up going nowhere.

Long-Term Goals Are Easier Than Short-Term

In my work as a success coach, I've found that for some women, their short-term goals are scarier than their big-picture vision.

This is especially true when it comes to money. Let me give you an example of this.

In one of the group coaching calls I host, my client Melissa got on the line and said she'd been really resistant to starting the work in the program; however, today she wanted to share one of her desires from Module 1. I invited Melissa to share and was excited to hear about what she'd uncovered.

Through a bit of obvious fear, she said, 'For a while, I've kind of thought – it feels even crazy saying it – that I want to be a billionaire. I want to have a billion dollars. If Oprah can do it, why can't I do it?'

I love hearing my clients proclaim their big-picture vision. Nothing makes me happier to hear a woman finally admitting what it is she desires – especially around money – and in such a public way. But at the same time, a red flag pops up for me when I hear statements like Melissa's. It wasn't that I doubted her dreams or whether she could really do it; it was about whether she was actually in reality about what she wanted, and what it was going to take to get there. After all, she'd admitted she was resistant even to getting started on Module 1 in the program!

Most people are hoping to achieve some sort of financial milestone – maybe it's six figures or the million-dollar goal. In Melissa's case, I could tell by her voice that there was a lot of shame and judgment coming up around her goal – and a lot of ambiguity. But when we looked deeper, it wasn't the big goal that was the problem: it was her current reality. Not only was she judging her big-picture goal, she was judging her current reality.

A young college professor getting her Ph.D in New York City, Melissa was living in a luxury apartment for which she paid $1,600 a month. She loved where she lived, but when people asked her how much rent she paid, she felt ashamed to admit it, and although she often shared the amount with them, she quickly mentioned that her job helped pay for a portion of the cost.

She felt like people would judge her for spending that amount of money, and didn't know if they would understand her dreams of living in the city. But the real truth was that she was judging herself above all else. That's the thing about judgment – if you're worried about what other people think or if others' opinions trigger or bother you, then you have to look inside and notice where you're also judging yourself or not living your truth.

Success Tip

If you're still wrestling with judgment around money, go back to the previous chapter and journal on what's coming up for you so you can release it.

Once we'd uncovered Melissa's judgment of herself, her current choices and her dreams, we were able to get to the root of what was going on. (Note: This is also a great example of how judgment blocks our desires!) I asked her to consider what it would take to get to that million- or billion-dollar level. She had no idea and was riddled with fear just thinking about it.

I shifted and asked her what her first goal was on the path to that destination. After some probing and number crunching, she figured out that her real-time goal was to make $2,000 a month in her new business. Then she'd be able to consider leaving her role as a professor – well, 'later on in the future,' she added.

As we spoke, it was obvious to me, and everyone else listening, that the $2,000 goal was far scarier to Melissa than her billion-dollar goal. Crazy, right? From the perspective of an outsider, that may make absolutely no sense. Of course, $2,000 is easier to earn than $2 billion or even $200,000. But think about it like this: big dreams are so far off in the future that they are the perfect excuse to not actually do anything to take action in the present moment.

For example, picture yourself driving to California for an interview. In NYC, you're safe. Around Ohio, you're still feeling pretty good. But by the time you get to Nevada, you're starting to freak out, realizing you're only a day away from your goal, and something is actually going to happen. Then what?

Your big-picture goals are out there waiting, perfectly taped to your vision board. They're far enough away that there's never any reason for you to make yourself feel bad for not having reached them.

In fact, big-picture dreams make you feel good about yourself because they automatically put you in the category of the driven, the dreamers, and those who are 'reaching for the stars.'

With big-picture goals, you feel like you don't actually have to do anything to get there – at least not yet.

But like so many others, you are lost in that fantasy and never actually do anything in the present moment. Because the goals are so far off in the future, you get to stay in your little bubble, believing everything you desire is on its way to you.

You're stuck in that belief to the degree that you're not taking action now, and never actually move forward toward that dream. And eventually, the dream doesn't feel so good anymore because nothing is actually happening. And when the brain starts to see that nothing's happening, eventually it lets go of the dream all together.

As motivational speaker Mel Robbins says, 'It's the small, ordinary, mundane kind of stuff that will set you on a path to success.' Once the brain sees you accomplishing these smaller tasks, it wants to keep repeating the process and get more pleasure.

You're not meant to have reached your big dreams yet. But that doesn't mean you don't have to start moving now.

In fact, it's essential that you *do* move now, and you can only do that by having short-term goals in place.

Focus on Today

My client Stacy lives in Houston and works as a high-school teacher. At the same time, she also makes costumes for the theater program at the school. As you can imagine, when it comes to her schedule, it's basically as if she has two jobs. Yet neither are what she actually wants to do.

On one of our coaching calls, Stacy shared that, like Melissa, she got really clear on her desires in the IHML program, and realized her real goal is to work for one of the professional theater companies in Houston and do their costume design as a freelancer. She also started a sewing blog and has big hopes for that as well.

She went on to say that she'd love season tickets to the theater – to be able to go to plays, ballets, and operas would be her version of massive success – and if she worked for one of the companies, she'd be gifted that opportunity. I could tell by her voice how much that vision excited her; yet at the same time, alarm bells were going off in my head. Stuck in the vision, I thought.

I told Stacy how much I loved hearing about her goals, and asked her whether she'd applied for a position at one of the theater companies yet. The other end of the line went silent, and I could feel her energy shift, even though we were 4,846 miles apart.

'No, I haven't. I don't think I could,' she replied, and then paused. 'Ugh, I just don't have the time.'

She caught herself: 'I know, I know – we make the time for the things we really want. But my time gets eaten up.'

'And why can't you go and freelance with them right now?' I asked. 'Have you applied or even gone to the theater to see if there are any opportunities available?'

'Not yet,' Stacy admitted.

'So how would it feel to do that?' I continued.

'Um, a little scary, but exciting,' she replied.

'In what way?'

'I'd have to deal with the rejection, if it came. Or if I actually got a position, I feel it would add a lot more to my plate. So it just...but…that's the kind of theater I actually want to design for – not for high school – so it would feel really exciting too.'

'Your job is to get excited about your desires,' I told her. 'It's not going to happen if you're scared of it happening and scared of it not happening. The Universe doesn't know what to do with that.'

I explained to Stacy that in order to move forward with her big-picture goals, she had to start taking action *today* on smaller goals. Otherwise, they could stay out in the ether, along with all the other un-actioned big dreams. I told her that I'm all about dreams being really big, and creating vision boards, but if you're not going to take action on them, they're a waste of time and energy. At the end of the call, Stacy finally got it and made a plan to take immediate action.

Get Detailed

It's possible for you to take immediate action too; however, in order to do so, you need to get really granular about what your actual goal is. In Stacy's case, she'd already taken one step forward in that she'd started her sewing blog. The next step was to make contact with the theaters. She could start by making a list of the companies she wanted to contact; then she could carve out an hour of her day to actually do that. She could also think about whether she already has contacts in the industry who could help her get a foot in the door.

Remember, this isn't about having the exact roadmap toward everything you want – none of us know exactly how we're going to get there. Think about someone you admire – I imagine they didn't have everything that's happened in their life completely mapped out (at least I don't think so!). That's not what I'm talking about here. What I am talking about is figuring out how to hit the $2,000 a month so you can hit six figures next year. And then take it from there.

By the way, I don't know what your specific goal is, so you'll have to be the one to map out the steps you want to start taking today. What I do know is that there isn't a 'right' way to do this, but there's probably a common way. So I highly recommend you speak to people who have done what it is you want to do and find a community of like-minded individuals and/or a mentor to guide you.

Play the Whole Tape Through

The other key element in successful goal-setting is connecting with how it would feel to reach that goal, and checking in with whether you think it's possible to achieve it. One of my coaches called this 'playing the whole tape through.' (We'll need to come up with a new phrase for future generations, who won't know what a cassette or VHS actually is, but it works for now!)

Playing the whole tape through means that when you make a goal – let's say to hit six figures – you ask yourself if you're willing to do whatever it takes to hit six figures. It sounds obvious, but this isn't a question most people ask. If you're not prepared to put in the effort and take action toward your goal, you're wasting your time and energy. I'm not saying you should throw the goal out the window completely, but I am saying you should revise it. You want to set yourself up for success, not failure. And remember, we aren't in the business of setting goals that end up just floating around.

If the goal is too big, or you don't feel you can reach it, then you won't.

This will leave you feeling frustrated, and potentially lower your confidence, which in turn will mean less action and goal-setting and fewer results going forward. This is why playing the whole tape through is so essential.

Let me give you another client example. Sharon took part in one of our masterminds for online entrepreneurs, and during a group session, she called in and asked for support in getting clear on her action steps and goals. She really wanted to start selling her new program designed for women who'd gone through a divorce, but thus far, she'd had people fill out consultation forms and either not show up for the call, or decide not to move forward with the coaching.

I could tell that Sharon, normally so levelheaded and calm, was frustrated and confused about how to change her current situation.

'How many clients do you want to come and register?' I asked her.

'Three in September,' she answered, without missing a beat.

'Okay, great. How many this month?' I went on. We were only one week into August.

'None this month,' Sharon said. She explained that she was in a new relationship and had her children home for the summer, so she didn't have time to take on any new clients. A red flag surfaced for me. In the moments before I'd started my line of questioning, Sharon had expressed frustration that she wasn't making any money that month.

'Well, that's why it's not happening!' I exclaimed, laughing. It clicked for her in that moment too. The reason she wasn't hitting her goal was because she didn't actually *want* to hit the goal. She hadn't played the whole tape through.

'You think?!' Sharon yelled into the phone.

'Yes, why would the Universe give you something you don't actually want?' I asked.

'I don't know whether to laugh or throw up,' Sharon replied.

The truth hit her right in the stomach. She said she even started to sweat when she realized what was going on beneath the surface. Sharon had subconscious programming running the show. Although she thought she wanted to sell her package, make money and move things forward in her business, her heart had a different agenda and wasn't actually on board with that goal. And she hadn't been aware of any of this until that moment. She was literally keeping herself stuck and stopping the sales from coming in, without knowing it. That's why it's so crucial that you get clear on what you want – in this moment *and* long term.

Goal-Setting as a Newbie

One of the questions I'm often asked by clients is how far out they should set their goals. Ninety days? Six months? A year? When it comes to specific goals, I highly recommend people take it month by month (this is what I did in the first 18 months of my business).

For example, ask yourself how much money you want to make this month. What personal goals do you want to reach? How do you want to transform your health? And then make sure that the goal contributes to the big-picture goals you also have in mind. There are a couple of reasons for doing this…

- **You want to set yourself up for success and small wins.** Once again, you don't want to be waiting to celebrate your successes. That doesn't feel good and it won't encourage you to continue to move forward.
- **You have no idea what you're capable of.** What if you're setting your goals too low? What if, by aiming for six figures by your 30th birthday, like I did, you're actually lowering the bar without knowing it and stunting your capability and growth?

By focusing on my own journey month by month, I was able to remain in the moment, and that meant all my energy and attention was going on the one single goal at hand. As you've probably noticed, my goals were connected to monetary amounts, but you should decide what works best for you.

Celebration Break

Let's take a second to celebrate everything you've learned about goal-setting so far. You now know how to set big-picture goals and simultaneously focus on the smaller, more immediate, goals that really matter when it comes to getting closer to your dreams. Woo hoo!

The Universe Has Your Back

For a second, forget everything I've just told you about goal-setting. Well, not really: but open your mind to the possibility that sometimes, you don't actually have to do anything but keep the faith and expect that things will turn out better than you could have imagined.

I see this all the time with my clients: once they get into momentum, doors open for them that they didn't expect. I share this to remind you that anything is possible. When you keep moving forward with your goals, you can achieve more than even you envisioned, and you can (and will) be surprised.

Quantum Leaps

Most of us assume that success is achieved one step at a time. This is another belief that's been instilled in us – and it's one that we can actually start to change to bring our dreams more rapidly into our reality. Simply put: it doesn't have to take as long as you think. You just have to keep moving forward, toward your desires, and trust that you're being supported. And it's not all down to you.

In his book *You²: A High Velocity Formula for Multiplying Your Personal Effectiveness in Quantum Leaps*, Price Pritchett says that 'right now… you are capable of exponential improvement in your performance. You can multiply your personal effectiveness,

Don't just put one foot in front of the other – take a quantum leap toward your dreams.

hit new highs and shatter your old achievement records…and become you squared.'[2]

What if you considered the idea that you don't just have to put one foot in front of the other – instead, you can take a quantum leap toward your dreams.

So, what if…

- You expected to knock your own socks off?
- You expected to do the impossible?
- You expected to shatter records?
- You realized you're capable of a quantum leap now?
- You just got started and didn't worry about the timeframe?
- You just showed up every day and gave your dreams your best?
- You doubled your goals or halved the time dedicated to reaching them?

Remember, *anything* is possible. I truly believe that, as Robin Sharma says, 'The future belongs to the misfits, oddballs and visionaries.'[3] So aim high. Expect more from yourself. This is your one life, so give it your all.

Action Step

Now that we've covered many of the key components in setting goals, it's time for you to map out your steps. What's your big-picture goal? Start with one. Then I highly recommend that you 'back into it' and lay out your 90-day and 30-day goals.

Next, ask yourself, what's the first step I can take in the direction of that goal? What can I do every day in order to reach it? At first, just listen to your intuition – what's it telling you? How have other people done what you want to do? And what is it going to take for you to reach that goal? Map out your steps and commit to taking them, starting today.

CHAPTER 7

Action

'Taking massive action on massive dreams amidst massive uncertainties, is pretty much where anyone who's ever done anything massive had to start. And then things got way easier.'[1]

MIKE DOOLEY

Between 2015 and 2016 I worked with hundreds of clients in my live programs, and even more went through my self-study courses. I hosted events and traveled around the world to be a part of masterminds and other group programs. I sent out an email every single Monday to my email list, ran Facebook ads, hosted teleclasses and live webinars, sent out more sales emails than I could count, and personally invited people to work with me.

The result? I was able to make seven figures in the first 18 months of my business. Seven figures! A million dollars in revenue. Once again, I tell you this so you can see what's possible for you too. (Clearly I did turn way more than my yearly salary into my monthly salary. Envision that for a second…)

I won the top award – the Divine Destiny award – at the group program I was a part of. James and I moved out of our tiny flat into one with four bedrooms, which meant we could each have an office. Oh, and that leads me to another milestone: James was able to resign from his 9–5 job and join me in the business as a coach.

We didn't plan on that happening; in fact, it was my coach who suggested it while I was with her in Bali. Thousands of miles apart, James and talked about it, and he put in his notice a week later. By April 2015, we were in Venice, celebrating him leaving his job and starting on this new adventure together.

By no means was this easy, but I did everything *I could think of doing and got out of my own way. I took more action than I ever had previously. I showed up, even when I didn't have confidence. I kept going, even when I was tired, scared, or unsure.*

And as a result of this combination of mindset + goals + action, I was able to transform my life. That's what's possible for you, too.

Mindset + Goals + Action

A key part of creating a life you love is owning your desires, admitting to having them, and then taking action toward them, and in this book, we've already explored a lot of the tips and tools for getting you there. However, I want you to understand that there's a chance your dreams will become pipe dreams if you're not taking action toward them.

If you look up the word 'pipe dream' in Urban Dictionary you'll see this definition: 'A vain dream that will never ever happen, given the harsh reality of life.'[2] That in itself is harsh! Back in Chapter 3, I shared that I believe your dreams and desires are literally 'dropped in' – that they are meant for you *and* possible. But the pipe dream risk is real; action is what stops your dream from becoming a pipe dream.

Think about it like this: all the money mindset work is great, all the goal-setting is admirable, but if you don't take the steps to *actually bring in the money*, you're probably not going to be any closer to the wealth and success you're craving. It may seem obvious to say this, but one of my biggest secrets to success is that I take more action than anyone I know. I show up – even when the fear is there (and it *is* there!)

Come Down Off the Mountaintop

I work with a lot of very spiritual women, and I'm spiritual myself – as you know, I believe the Universe has my back, and I'm all about the power of silence and meditation. I definitely think we should 'feel' into what we want and what that right next step is for us, but at the same time, I know that we have to take action on behalf of our dreams.

The mistake I see so many women make is going to that spiritual 'mountaintop' – whether it's meditation, a retreat, or journaling – and staying up there for far too long.

Mel Robbins illustrates the importance of taking action in one of my favorite quotes: 'You may never feel inspired or clear-headed enough to seize a moment, but you have to force yourself to do it even if you don't want to... The best time to act on a feeling you have is right now.'[3]

Mel created the powerful '5 Second Rule,' which suggests you take action on a feeling or thought within five seconds (otherwise you never will, due to your head getting in the way.) Think about it – how often is your heart saying 'yes' in terms of your dreams but then your head butts in and allows fear to run the show?! This chapter is about getting you to take massive action on behalf of your dreams, and that requires you to come down off the mountaintop.

On the flip side, I've also worked with women who are such huge action-takers that they do far too much at any one time and end up overcommitted. That's definitely been one of my personal struggles. In fact, in the beginning of building my business, my coach flat-out told me I was showing up like I had four months left to live. She was right. I'm a doer.

In 2015, there came a point when I was working 80–100 hours a week on running two group programs and working with 27 clients one-on-one, and I was also traveling around the world. I remember telling my coach (through tears) on one of our calls that I just wanted to be able to see my husband. She promised me that there was light at the end of the tunnel, but also encouraged me not to take on so many things at once.

Although working in that way brought in a lot of money for my company, I knew it wasn't sustainable. This chapter is not about the promotion of burnout, but it is about showing up on behalf of your dreams through taking action toward your goals.

Know What Action to Take

When I interviewed my friend Bob Heilig, an incredible seven-figure entrepreneur, for my *I Heart My Life Show*, he talked about the amount of action and implementation he takes. He said people always think that because he's taking such fast action, he's really clear about what he's doing and what's going to work. But the truth is, it's the complete opposite – because he's not sure, he takes action quickly so he can pivot if necessary. I can definitely relate to that.

The truth is: it can be difficult to know which steps will lead to the result you want. For example, going back to our analogy of traveling across the United States using Google Maps, there are thousands of routes you could take to get from New York to LA – and it's the same with your dreams.

However, just like that cross-country journey, when we're clear on our goals, have a starting place in mind and an ultimate destination (or at least an idea of the area we want to end up), it's really just about putting one foot in front of the other.

Why Do We Procrastinate?

Just like understanding how your mind works and how to handle fear and worry, I want you to know there will be times when you won't want to take action because you don't 'feel' like it. In fact, there will be days when every fiber of your being will tell you to stay curled up in your bed and to put off until tomorrow that next step toward your dreams. But here's the key: if you're ready to make your dreams a reality, you can't wait until the mood strikes or you have 100 percent clarity.

To paraphrase the US poet Ralph Waldo Emerson: do the thing, and you will have the power to do the thing. Think about working out – once you get to the gym or to the yoga class, you feel proud of yourself; you get into the mindset of being there and take the action required. But lacing up those training shoes and getting out the door often feels like a struggle.

Brendon Burchard spent years studying success and this is demonstrated beautifully (and quite impressively) in his book *High Performance Habits*. When it comes to wanting to take action, he says that you won't be overcome every day with magical waves of inspiration. You won't necessarily feel 'in the mood' to write your program content, to work on your website, or to invest in your business. You have to consistently generate the desire to do it. As he says, 'the energy plant doesn't have energy, it generates it.'[4]

Find Your 'Why'

In those moments when you don't feel like moving forward or taking action, your first step is to keep in mind your *why*. Ask yourself *why* it's so important that you create or grow your business (for example). Is it to create a better life for yourself and your family? Is it so you can have the kind of opportunities you've been longing for? Or be able to make an impact in the world?

Everyone's *why* is different. For instance, when it comes to losing weight, some people do it so they can fit into their clothes; others want to feel stronger, lower their risk for disease and have more energy; others still want some time away from the kids. You get the idea.

My *why* was always financial freedom and making an impact. For example, back when I was getting my business off the ground, James and I went to a house party, and after about two hours, I started to get the itch to leave.

But I felt guilty. What would people think? What would James think? But I remember thinking to myself that I would soon be able to invite people to a much better party if I continued to move forward and dedicated myself to my vision. (Just being honest – we were in a crappy flat drinking crappy beer with people I wasn't even close to!) So I told James that I was headed home, and jumped on the train back to our flat to work on my business. And a few years later, we were able to throw an incredible Christmas party, complete with a private chef!

Remembering your *why* is crucial in helping you move forward when faced with those less-than-inspiring moments. When you keep your purpose at the forefront, regardless of your mood or your feelings when you wake up each day, you'll be reminded of what motivates you to take that next step in the direction of your dreams. Let your *why* serve as a reminder that you already have the ability within you to take at least one action step today that will bring you closer to the life and success you desire.

Success Tip

Write down your *why* and keep it in a place where you'll see it often – on your nightstand, your bathroom mirror, or your laptop. Use it as a way to begin each day with a reminder of why taking action matters. Let it serve as inspiration for setting an intention for your day.

What Is Procrastination Giving You?

The next step is to ask yourself what you're *getting* from procrastination. (Remember, there's always a reason why we're continuing to show up and not show up in a certain way.) The answer might shock you. You may hear things like, *It keeps me safe*, *No one will make fun of me*, or *I can't get it wrong*.

There's always a deeper reason behind why we do something... and why we don't.

It's your job to uncover that motive and shift it. And as luck would have it, the best way to shift it is through action! Decide to move forward in spite of your mood or your feelings. Even when the mood isn't striking, use your reasons for doing what you're doing as your motivation to create something, to sell something, and to propel your dreams forward.

Trust me, I know what it's like to have those days when things feel less than inspiring. But I've learned that when I take action in spite of 'not feeling like it' I *really* start to build momentum, to create resilience within myself, and to form the habit of being persistent. I become disciplined.

(By the way, discipline doesn't have to mean what you think it does – getting yelled at and punished by your parents or the teachers at school. It means that you're a 'disciple of' something. I'm a disciple of life, of writing, of coaching, of inspiration. And that discipline has been key to my taking action and setting myself apart from the crowd.)

You have what it takes to do that too. You have the ability to make your dreams your reality. So make the commitment to yourself right now to take action and move forward toward your dreams, each and every day. Because you and your dreams are worth that effort.

Stop Waiting for Perfect

As a driven woman, you may be tempted to put off taking any action until you feel like you have everything together – i.e. you have an amazing website, you have the qualification framed on your wall, you have a beautiful workspace, and so on. If that's you today, just know that this is totally natural. But as someone once said to me, perfectionism is just like procrastination, but in a cuter outfit.

Our ego tells us that if we don't have everything figured out, it must mean we're not ready. This is something I hear constantly from my clients. They want everything to be perfect before they start – the perfect time, the perfect amount of money in the bank account, the perfect strategy for success. But there are two issues here:

1. Perfect doesn't exist. Just as when you plan to have a baby or move home, there's never a perfect time.
2. The thought that one of those perfect moments exists means we're left waiting and never actually get those qualifications, or take the action needed to move toward our goals.

The reality is that everyone who's amazing at something was once a total beginner at it, and the only reason they're now skilled and rockin' it is because they didn't wait on perfection – they took action and learned and grew as they went along.

My motto is: If it's in your heart, you're ready to start. Period. No one starts out being incredible at something or having everything 'together' from the get-go. The people who go on to become masters and pros don't keep waiting: they take action, fumble their way through, and make their dreams their reality.

Perfect Is Boring

I'm not sure where the memo that perfect = successful comes from (especially for women), but I now know it's actually not

My motto is:
If it's in your heart,
you're ready to start.

true – particularly when it comes to going for your dreams. As a society, we've turned a corner, with the rise of plus-size influencers and curvier models becoming more prevalent in fashion campaigns.

And if you look closely, our favorite TV characters aren't perfect, either. People don't want perfect. Take our beloved *Friends* characters: Ross, Rachel, Phoebe, Chandler, Monica, and Joey. They've been wildly popular for decades, yet they're flawed, just like you and me. It's their non-perfect traits – Phoebe being wacky, Joey being well, not the smartest, and Monica being neurotic – that make us love them and relate to them.

It's the same for you, especially if you're someone who is building a brand or business – people want the real deal. They want to be able to relate to you, and that's not possible if you're constantly showing up as perfect. Because *they* aren't perfect. No one is.

I know this may sound strange coming from a girl who wears Kate Spade and poses in front of the Eiffel Tower with her beautiful British husband, but hear me out. There's a difference between having high standards and aiming toward perfect. The latter means action isn't taken because you're constantly trying to reach something that doesn't exist, and it's a huge waste of energy and your talents.

Just like worry, my own quest for perfection has only ever given me anxiety, worry, tears, time wasted, a delay in results, putting too much on my plate, overeating, and even back pain. On the other hand, having high standards *but moving forward despite things not being perfect*, has given me oh so many positives: the chance to work with and affect extraordinary women around the world; getting my brand and message out there; celebrating five- and six-figure months; taking trips around the world; having the support of an incredible team; forming amazing friendships; and getting to collaborate with spectacular mentors.

See what I mean? Although letting go of perfect is still a work in progress for me, I know now that I'm never going to get to where I want to go, or be happy along the journey, if I'm always going for perfect. So what about you?

- Are you waiting until the timing is 'perfect' before you start your dream business?
- Are you waiting to step on stage until you have that 'perfect' message?
- Are you stalling going for that promotion until you're 'perfectly' qualified?
- Are you still trying to do everything yourself 'perfectly' instead of outsourcing it?

How about taking imperfect action instead? How about deciding that you know enough, are ready enough and are skilled enough? Because it's true – you are enough. You are perfect the way you are, and the world needs you out there today.

Celebration Break

Perfect isn't necessary. You're ready now. Let's do this!

You May Not Be Ready (But Who Cares?!)

A few years ago, one of my clients told me that she didn't even design her wedding flower arrangements without first getting the qualification to do so. I had to laugh, but there's another part of me that finds it so sad that we're holding ourselves back because we don't feel ready or aren't yet qualified.

You aren't to blame for this. We were taught that we need a piece of paper to do anything grand, but unless you're planning to become one of the world's top surgeons, I want you to really evaluate what you do truly need to make your dreams a reality. Is it a degree? Or is that just a delaying tactic? Is it the fear talking? You have to learn how to differentiate between waiting because you're delaying and waiting because it truly isn't the right time.

You may need and want more experience in order to reach your dreams, and you may be right in thinking it will help your mission. However, I want you to give yourself permission to get started today, whether you have the experience or not. Because the truth is, experience is the best way to learn and the fastest path to the qualification you're looking for. And it may not come in the form of a degree or a piece of paper. (What if you qualified yourself instead?)

Stop Waiting

As I explained earlier, when I began my business as a coach, I focused on working with women experiencing the ups and major downs of a quarter-life crisis. They knew they were meant for something big, but didn't know how to make it happen. I didn't start out as a business or a success coach, because I myself wasn't there yet. But as I gained momentum and my business grew, my expertise also expanded and I was able to work with a wider variety of clients.

So, although it's important to make sure you're in alignment with the work you're doing in the world, and 'qualified' to do so, make sure you're not a chronic waiter. Because the thing is, you're never going to get more experience unless you actually start.

Waiting is an epidemic among women, and it's killing our dreams and causing sadness and frustration.

An article called 'The Confidence Gap' published in the *Atlantic* magazine illustrates this phenomenon beautifully. Its authors explain how the computer hardware company Hewlett-Packard was trying to work out how to get more women into top management positions and decided to review its HR records. It discovered that its male employees were prepared to apply for a promotion if they felt they met 60 percent of the job's requirements, whereas the women applied only when they met 100 percent of them.[5]

In further documenting this 'waiting epidemic,' the authors point out that studies have found that 'men overestimate their abilities and performance, and women underestimate both. Over-qualified and over-prepared, too many women still hold back.'[6] The conclusion: stop waiting.

Get into Action

If you're ready to start, do it. Just know that the mastery will come in time. You'll learn more as you go along. You'll need to reevaluate as you go along. Remember, waiting just gives you more of the same, and often times, it's a delaying tactic instigated by the ego. It's like having one foot in and one foot out. You're better than that. Ask yourself what you're missing out on by waiting. Ask yourself who's missing out on you. What impact are you not having by waiting? How are you (and your family) suffering? It's time to take action instead.

Move Forward with Your Dreams

Here are a few tools for showing up big time on behalf of your dreams: use this list whenever you need a quick reminder and inspiration to take action.

1. Stop dabbling.

2. Make quick decisions.

3. Be consistent.
4. Show up.
5. Use every second.
6. Go the extra mile.
7. Just ask.
8. Have faith.

Now let's take an in-depth look at each of these ideas.

1. Stop Dabbling

One of my clients recently shared that she was 'so close to being committed' to her goals. I asked her what that actually meant. (In my mind, it meant the same thing as *not* being committed.)

You see, so often we fall into the trap of dabbling. We think that if we put a little bit of effort in, we won't have to fully commit, and most of the time, showing up like that means fear is running the show. You're worried what will happen if you *do* commit. What if it doesn't work out? Or what if it does? Sometimes that's just as scary.

What if people laugh at you or judge you? What if you do become wildly successful and lose all your friends and family because they think you're too full of yourself and too obsessed with money? Trust me, I've heard (and felt) it all.

Just as we discussed in previous chapters though, we cannot allow our fears and worries to get the better of us and stop us from living our dreams, or to keep our dreams in pipe-dream status. Believe me, this is not a one-and-done practice. As you up-level in life, your career or business, you will have to regularly check in to see if you're really 'all in.'

For example, at the time of writing this book, I had dinner with one of my good friends – she is very well known in the coaching industry and was in the midst of making some changes in her business and shifting direction. We sat on a gorgeous terrace in London and she told me she was just going to 'dip her toe in the water' with her new program. My BS (bullshit) meter was at an all-time high on that day and was going off as she spoke. I just looked at her with an expression that let her know she wasn't fooling me.

'What?' she asked.

'You're ready now,' I said.

She went quiet for a bit. 'I guess I just wonder if I'm worthy.'

I had a similar conversation with one of my clients, who was also showing up in a half-assed way. I simply asked her what it would look like for her to be 'all in.' That shifted everything for her.

Are you being called toward something? Is your intuition telling you to take that step? Then you're ready! Think about a baby learning to walk. It has no idea what it's doing; it just starts. It follows its intuition to crawl and then stand up and then walk. And it isn't perfect at all. It's wobbly, it's messy, there are tears, but there are also major triumphs. The world opens up for that baby. That's what's possible for you.

As Iyanla Vanzant says in her book *Trust*, 'we take out first breath outside of the womb because something within us trusts that the next breath will come with grace and ease. Babies do not think or talk themselves out of their needs; babies do not believe their needs are wrong.[7]

At what point do we stop trusting our instincts that are telling us that now is the time to act? And if you can't hear that voice anymore, at what point did you let fear cover it up so it's no longer audible? Without action – without starting before you're ready – there's no chance for change. And you're meant for so much more than that.

By the way, even a small action is better than no action at all. So if you're feeling stuck in a rut or unworthy, take action. Learn something. Try something new. Put yourself out there. There's no better time than now to start truly embracing your potential and pursuing your passions. There's no reason to put your desires on hold any longer. After all, one small step can be all it takes to start walking in the direction of your dreams. As Stacey, one of my previous clients, says: JFDI. Just F*cking Do It.

2. Make Quick Decisions

In his classic 1937 book *Think and Grow Rich*, Napoleon Hill said: 'Successful people make decisions quickly (as soon as all the facts are available) and change them very slowly (if ever). Unsuccessful people make decisions very slowly, and change them often and quickly.'[8] In my experience, it's not the fast decision-making alone that makes you successful – it's the fact that when you make quicker decisions, you actually make more decisions and take more action. (Just like Bob described earlier in this chapter.) You also lose less energy on worry and the bouncing back and forth between action and no action.

Think about your body, the energy coursing through it up and down. You wake up in the morning and it's filled to the brim with energy. As you start your day, maybe you lose some energy on deciding what to wear or what to eat for breakfast. (You may have heard about people like Einstein wearing the same clothes day after day? There's a reason for that – decisions can be draining.) Then you lose a bit more deciding which route to take to work or what project to start on. These are simple examples, but I want you to start to recognize when you're spending too much time in limbo land and aren't getting enough done.

Limbo land is where dreams go to die.

You go round and round about something until you *have* to make a decision because you've no more energy to think about it (and you really need all that energy to achieve what you want to achieve!) And then it's over and you're in a worse place than where you started! Here are a few other key elements to making quick decisions:

Without action -
without starting
before you're ready -
there's no chance
for change.

Focus on Where You Want to Be

I help my clients make decisions based on where they want to be, not from where they currently are. (Note: this is especially important on sales calls. As you know, there was a period of time when I had 54 'nos' in a row, and I had to face the fact that I wasn't so great at sales. And why would I have been, since I'd never done it before? I discovered that, as a coach, one of the biggest shifts I had to make was to learn how to help a potential client make a decision. Most people don't know how to make a decision, so helping them do so is a game-changer. For that reason, whenever I'm on sales calls with potential clients, I do my best to help them make a decision about moving forward, there and then on the phone. Whether it's working with me or not, it doesn't matter. No one likes to end up in limbo land because literally nothing happens there besides the draining of your energy.)

It's my job to help my clients connect with their heart and what they actually want, and make a decision based on where they want to be – not from where they currently are. I hope this resonates with you too. So many of us are making decisions based on our current reality – I don't have the money so I can't sign up; the trip isn't possible so I'm not going to book the hotel or even do the research; I can't coach so I'd better not even try.

As you know, our mind often pulls from our past to predict our future, which is often why we're so scared to move forward. Our brain is hardwired to function on autopilot, based on what we've experienced in the past – which is another reason why it's so common for us to feel resistance and fear when trying to start something new. And all too often, I see women get stuck in that place of resistance because they're looking backward instead of looking ahead. That's why it's essential to realize that looking ahead is a deliberate choice and central to taking the right action on behalf of your dreams.

For example, when I was starting out in my business, I had to consciously make the decision to let go of limiting beliefs from my past (for instance, my money story, the times when I'd failed at something, or the idea that I was too late) and instead choose to look ahead and imagine a new picture of what was possible. I could no longer base my idea of what was possible on what I'd experienced or been taught in the past.

And I've since learned that gaining momentum in life and business is all about making decisions from where you want to be, not from where you are now or where you've been.

It's so powerful when you make decisions based on what you desire, not on your current state.

An example of this would be buying the domain name, moving forward with the coaching program, going to the event. Implement this, and your whole life will change.

Make Your Decisions Right

I also recommend that you avoid 'buyer's remorse' when it comes to your decisions. We've all been there – you make a decision and then all of a sudden your ego tries to get you to go back on it. In those moments when it seems like things aren't working out, we often wonder if we're going to get it wrong.

One of my mentors once asked me how it would feel to make all my decisions right, and to recognize that there really isn't a wrong decision. I've implemented that concept in my life and business. Although I still get tripped up from time to time, I now know that the moments when I don't trust myself are the ones that make decision-making more difficult. How free would you feel if from now on, you made all your decisions right, and knew that no matter what the outcome, you've got this?

Make More Decisions

Making quick decisions also means that you make more decisions and take more action over a period of time, which results in more failures but also more successes. It's a numbers game. I'm not saying you should be hasty, but when we wait and go back and forth around decisions, our mind tends to take over and we forget what we actually want. It's as if we can't hear our heart anymore.

Think about the last time you had an important decision to make. I imagine you knew the right answer from the start, but you allowed your mind to delay you, or even to talk you out of it. You want to avoid limbo land, and making decisions quickly helps you do that.

3. Be Consistent

I've mentioned a few times the group program I was part of when I started out as a coach; this was instrumental in helping me move forward with my dreams. It taught me the ins and outs of business and mindset, and provided me with incredible connections with like-minded women.

However, one of the interesting things I started to notice within the group is that not everyone had what it takes to run a business and achieve their goals. Of course it was humanly possible for them, but when it came to taking action and being consistent, it was a constant dance of one step forward, two steps back. The truth is, anyone is capable of starting and taking action in the beginning, but you have to be in it for the long term. As Robin Sharma says: 'Consistency is the mother of mastery.'[9]

Take a marital relationship for example: anyone can date, be infatuated, spend every waking hour with their new love – but how many people are in it for the long haul? How many people are willing to put in the work? How many are willing to commit to the relationship during the good, the bad and the ugly?

It's like this with your dreams. When it comes to taking action, are you dedicated or dabbling? Is it two steps forward and one step back? Is it consistent action one week and then take the next week off?

Recently, one of my previous clients sent me a message saying: 'Your dedication is really inspiring... I was thinking about it the other day: how you just stick to what you're doing, no matter what it takes, what anyone thinks, or where the "market" goes. And that is amazing.'

Over the years, quite a few IHML community members who have been following me from the beginning have told me they admire and value my consistency. I've written a newsletter every Monday since I started – that's several years' worth of emails. I remember hearing Marie Forleo say that unless the Internet is dead or she's dead, her followers are going to hear from her every Tuesday! What if *you* showed up like that? How would things change?

When it comes to taking action, are you consistent? Are you dedicated to your vision? Or are you making excuses, not showing up, and not being willing to give it 100 percent? If it's the latter, it's crucial that you commit to changing that today. You can't show up for 50 percent of the time and expect to get massive results.

Think about it like this: if you only ate healthily for 50 percent of the time, how would you expect your body to feel? If you only disciplined your kids for 50 percent of the time, would they trust your rules? If you only showed love to your partner for 50 percent of the time, would they know you cared for them? (Maybe a little, but you get the idea!)

4. Show Up

There will be times in your life when you just have to move forward, despite things not being perfect (or even close to it!) In fact, I didn't quite know the direction my business was headed in the beginning – I was still figuring everything out. But I did know how badly I wanted to get clients and grow my business, because it was my passion and I knew I could help people.

And I realized that I had to keep putting myself out there and being persistent – even if that meant taking sales calls on a random park bench in California! (One of the two potential clients did sign up, so it was worth it.) I had to keep showing up; I had to make my presence known. I had to show everyone, myself and the Universe that I was in this for the long haul.

5. Use Every Second

Since starting my business, every time I've sat in a nail or hair salon, I've used the time to finish tasks for my company – answering emails, writing funnels, responding to clients, writing programs, working on my website: you name it, I've done it in a salon – or I've gone deeper with my personal development game by reading or listening to audios.

Every single appointment, the staff ask me if I want a magazine, and every single time I say, 'No thanks: I've brought my computer' or 'No thanks: I've brought my book.' Believe me, I love reading *People* magazine as much as the next girl, but while others are reading it, I'm thinking about how I can appear in it. Those epic 3–4 hour hair appointments (you blondes can relate to this!) have sparked some mega results.

Although I walked through that salon door for some sort of external transformation, the truth is that from those chairs, I've created a movement and transformed myself from the inside out as well, and I've made a ton of money. People ask me how I've been able to create what I've built in the past few years. This is how: I've dedicated myself to the vision. And that means using my time wisely – every single second of it.

Don't misunderstand me here: I'm not saying we always have to be doing something – after all, moments of silence and stillness are valuable too – but how much more productive would you be if you actually took advantage of your time? How much could you accomplish in between appointments? While you're waiting for dinner to cook in the oven? While you're sitting outside the dressing room as your partner tries on clothes at the store? Getting your hair done?

We all have the same number of hours in our day as Beyoncé, Sara Blakely (who has four kids!), and anyone else you admire. Just sayin'.

Is it time to drop the 'I don't have the time' excuse and find the time instead?

You have so much more time than you know. You just have to be aware of every spare moment. Recognize the opportunity to move forward and seize it. Be disciplined. Decide to take action.

Success Tip

Think about how you're spending your time. For example, the average American adult watches 4.3 hours of TV per day[10] Seriously?! There are shows I love to watch as well, but if you fall into that camp, let's be real here: *you have time.*

6. Go the Extra Mile

One of the entrepreneurs I follow on Instagram is Jesse Itzler, husband of Sara Blakely. Jesse is a serial entrepreneur with a net worth of $200 million. I love following him and Sara on their journey with their kids and multiple companies.

One of Jesse's posts, which featured a photo of him on the basketball court with other 40-something men, really caught my attention. The caption read: 'You don't have to be the most talented… just find your point of differentiation.'

Jesse went on to describe a period of time when he was part of a '40 and over' basketball tryout. There were 70 people trying out for six spots. In order to help them prep, the coach sent them a suggested workout program to get them in shape and ensure they'd be tryout-ready. Jesse read the instructions and figured that if he did the exact program he'd been sent, he'd be in the exact same shape as everyone else. So what did he do? He doubled it.

For 45 days he did 'almost puke' workouts on the dirt road behind his house. On the day of the tryouts, he took it one step further and decided to pair with the man who'd been the best on the team the previous year. Six minutes into the game, that player had his hands on his knees and was gasping for air. Jesse wrote that in that moment, he thought to himself, *He wasn't on that dirt road with me*. He wasn't on that dirt road doing the almost-puke workouts. He wasn't taking the same action. He wasn't as 'all in.'

Jesse ended the post with the words 'Same Rule Applies in Business'! I couldn't agree more. In working with entrepreneurs and driven women, I see a lot of patterns – stopping when things get difficult; not going the extra mile; expecting success to be handed over on a silver platter; backing off when fear shows up; following the crowd.

Jesse hit the nail on the head with this post: going above and beyond is key to success. You have to stand out and go the extra mile. It's so important to be you and do what you love because that will set you apart from the crowd. Think about what would happen if you doubled your efforts. What if you got up an hour earlier? What if you did one more video? What if you doubled the number of people you told about your program?

The truth is that most people aren't consistently taking action; most people aren't showing up every day; most people aren't actually willing to work hard. Like I said, I recognized this in my own life. More than 200 people went through the group program I was a part of. Do you know how many are actually really successful today? Maybe 10 percent – and that's being generous. This has nothing to do with the program itself: people just stop too soon. You know the saying 'Go the extra mile, it's never crowded?' There's a reason it exists! Along my own journey, I saw people dropping off, giving up, not trusting that they were capable.

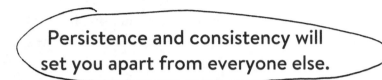

Persistence and consistency will set you apart from everyone else.

There's a graphic I love that illustrates this truth perfectly. It shows the juxtaposition between the miner who keeps going and eventually finds the diamonds, and the one who turns around too soon, even though the diamonds are right on the other side of the next portion of wall. Keep going – the diamonds are there.

7. Just Ask

When James and I got engaged, we naturally started to think about the location for our wedding. One evening while we were hanging out at our flat, I told him I wanted to check out The Ritz Hotel in London. I still remember that look he gave me – the one he still uses when his wife comes up with crazy ideas; only now he's not surprised! 'We could never afford that,' he said.

From an external perspective, his belief was completely justified. But I knew that it didn't hurt to ask. What was the worst that could happen? They'd email us back, telling us the price and confirming it was out of our budget? Or maybe we'd have a meeting with them, getting to spend an hour in a beautiful hotel and have a glass of champagne? I operate with the belief that it doesn't hurt to ask.

Think about your own life and goals – how many times have you missed out on an opportunity because you didn't ask? It could be as big as getting the wedding venue of your dreams or as small as getting what you really want at a restaurant, even though it's not actually on the menu. The worst thing that could happen is that someone says 'no.' And is that *really* the worst thing? Would you really not be able to handle that? (The answer to that question is also 'no' by the way.)

You can start practicing this today with something small: ask the smoker sitting next to you to move away; ask the waiter to bring you another glass of wine because the one you have right now isn't what you wanted; ask the man out on the date. You get the idea. Those are just simple examples, but they can give you the courage to be bold when it comes to your dreams. After all, don't they deserve that?

8. Have Faith

Remember when I got on a call with my coach and told her it wasn't working? I was really down in the dumps, thinking that nothing was happening. I could have been one of the ones who didn't make it. I could have given up. Thank goodness she reminded me what I was meant for and what was possible. She had faith when I didn't.

One of the phrases Brendon Burchard uses with his clients and in his teachings is 'honor the struggle.' There will be struggle. There will be challenge, but you have to keep showing up. Just as an airplane uses the majority of its fuel while taking off, you getting your dreams off the ground is going to take a massive amount of action and energy; there's no other way to say it.

But that's how it's supposed to be! Remember, you're like a woman in labor – you're literally birthing a new life – but it won't be like this forever. It's the same with weight loss – if you're looking to transform the composition of your body, it's going to take a lot of effort. But then, once the weight is off, you move into maintenance phase.

There's a reason why they say success and failure live on the same street. You're so close. Keep going!

The Quality of Your Action

The final thought I want to leave you with in this chapter is to pay attention to the quality of your action. Ask yourself whether there's an intention behind the steps you're taking. I'm not saying you're always going to know how something will pan out, but I am saying that you should give it your all regardless.

Remember the old phrase 'How you do one thing is how you do everything'? It may sound silly but how are you making the bed? How are you cooking dinner? How are you exercising? Are you all in? Or are you dabbling? And are you taking action that's going to get you closer to the life you want? Is it *intentional* action? Pay attention to the quality of your action when you're going for your dreams and everything will shift.

Action Step

What action are you going to take on behalf of your dreams? Remind yourself of your short-term goals and make a list of all the actions you're going to take on behalf of those goals. How are you going to remain consistent and bold?

CHAPTER 8

Self

'Love yourself first and everything else falls into line. You really have to love yourself to get anything done in this world.'[1]

LUCILLE BALL

The action I took in the first few years of building my business led to some incredible results. In particular, 2016 brought new waves of opportunities and excitement in our lives and business. Just scrolling through my iPhone photos from that year reveals exactly that. In order to juxtapose what I'm about to share in this chapter, I wanted to list out what 2016 consisted of, so here goes (I promise, there's a point)…

1. *James and I started the year by extending our New Year's trip to Vail Ski Resort by a few weeks, just because we wanted to (we even flew my best friend out there to join us).*

2. *I traveled to New York (twice) to mingle with top influencers, host an event and have a photoshoot.*

3. *James was officially certified as a High Performance Coach.*
4. *We took romantic trips to Spain and Florida.*
5. *We hosted clients in Paris, where I bought my first Chanel necklace.*
6. *We moved into an even bigger house in London – this time it had six bedrooms and the most gorgeous bathroom you ever did see.*
7. *We celebrated my birthday first in California, with friends who flew in from all over the world, and then in Paris at the newly renovated Ritz Paris Hotel, where I bought my second Chanel necklace.*
8. *We both signed up for a $60,000 mastermind with Brendon Burchard.*
9. *We hosted another event in London for our clients.*

You get the idea… life was good. From the outside looking in, everything was exactly as it was always meant to be. And by all accounts, it looked like I really did love my life. How could I not? And to be honest, I really thought I did.

In December 2016, I attended the Titan Summit, hosted by Robin Sharma. The four days were filled with lots of 'ahas' and the world's most amazing and inspirational speakers. On the third day of the conference, we were in the middle of completing an exercise when Robin posed us a question that would change me forever. Although he was speaking to the room, I felt like he was talking just to me. He asked, 'Are you happy?'

I'm sure that question doesn't sound particularly riveting, but for me in that moment, it was powerful because of what I heard next.

No. No. No.

I was stunned. I immediately thought about my current reality. It was so different to where I'd been just a few years earlier. I'd hit seven figures; I was in a room with billionaires; I had amazing clients; our house was incredible; I was working with the love of my life. What more could I want?

It's confusing when you get what you want and find that you're still not happy. After all, during my quarter-life crisis, I'd been so sure that when my vision board manifested into a new reality, I'd finally have nothing to worry about. So what went wrong?

I *Should* Heart My Life, Right?

Let's be clear about one thing: I knew I couldn't *not* love my life. I ran a company called I Heart My Life, after all. I felt guilty that I wasn't happy. I was embarrassed. After all, so much of what I wanted had come to fruition. Nothing was inherently wrong with my life, and I was incredibly blessed. But none of that seems to matter if you wake up one day and realize that your life has been a whole series of *waiting* for things to get good. Although I won't pretend to know what it's like to have a child of my own, I felt like a mother who births a new life and is so engrossed in raising her child that she forgets about herself. My business, in fact, had taken over.

What would make me 'happy'? Would I ever be happy? Would my dial ever turn to happy? I needed to find out. It was time to recalibrate.

Happiness = Self-Love

Simply put, what I soon realized was that, ultimately, increasing my happiness meant increasing my self-love (or my focus on self).

In working with two coaches over a period of nine months, I learned there were some key concepts I had yet to master that were negatively affecting my happiness: health, boundaries, anxiety, presence, saying 'no', pressure, trust, foresight, among others. Ultimately, all of them had to do with me putting myself first and experiencing ultimate self-love.

I also began to see that neither happiness nor self-love are by-products of success – just like other key elements of success, they too have to be generated and focused on. They aren't always naturally occurring, and it isn't usual for women like us to put ourselves first. In fact, as one of my coaches used to describe it: we often leave ourselves the crumbs. And for many of us, it takes an experience like the one I shared above to act as a wakeup call to the reality that we can no longer put ourselves last, or expect to just 'feel' happy.

Self-love and happiness are not by-products of success – they too have to be generated and focused on.

Put Your Own Oxygen Mask on First

Think about it like this: when we're on a plane, there's a reason why we're instructed to fasten our oxygen mask before helping others, but we rarely do this in everyday life. This chapter is about helping you learn how to do that for yourself. As the Dalai Lama said: 'The world will be saved by the Western woman.'[2] But that can't happen if you're in a coffin, burnt out, or consistently so self-sacrificing that you have no energy to live your purpose.

Before we really dive in, know that this chapter is a miracle in itself. I never envisioned myself writing it. Self-love in particular wasn't part of my former recipe for success. I was of the mindset that tough love and harsh 'motivating' words are what is required. The fact that I was even at the Titan Summit, having that wakeup call, was a miracle as well. I'd bought the $7,500 ticket on a whim on my phone when I'd first heard Robin speak. I knew I had to be in that room, but I wasn't expecting to learn that I was unhappy.

And if that's where you're at today – with the connection between self-love and success not yet made – I invite you to remain open. Even if you're not ready for what I'm sharing, know it's here waiting for you when you are. It's been a learning curve for me too, but once I really got this, everything changed and I was able to discover what would not only create *sustainable* success, but consistent happiness as well. And isn't that why we're all really here after all?

From where I sit today, I see that I'm blessed to be one of those people who have had a radical wakeup call that resulted in a personal quest for joy and ultimately love of self. I'm going to share some of the top shifts that helped me transform my life and get me loving it (maybe for the first time).

Celebration Break

We're part of a movement of women who are no longer willing to put themselves last. (Trust me, the world doesn't need another example of a woman leaving herself with the crumbs.) That deserves some major celebration!

Make Happiness the Goal

Like many of the topics we've already covered in this book, happiness isn't something we're taught in school. And although I believe we're born joyful, we lose sight of that joy along the way. We lose sight of ourselves. We get so wrapped up in the external that we forget to look within.

We look outside of ourselves for the answers. We see others doing what we desire to do and think their way is the recipe for success, and we should follow it. I'm not saying that's wrong or that you need to reinvent the wheel entirely, but you need to put your own spin on it and create your version of what that success looks like – with the focus on happiness first and foremost.

For example, most of our clients come to us desiring freedom, and I always ask them to explain what that really means to them because everyone's definition is different. It's the same with happiness, and I think we're always rewriting that definition. It can evolve and change as we go along.

I've seen in my own life the power of happiness, and doing what feels good to me versus what I think I 'should' be doing. If happiness isn't a part of our everyday life, why are we doing what we're doing? What's the point?

We live in a 'I'll be happy when…' world. For example, 'I'll feel more fulfilled, happy, and confident when I get my business off the ground'; 'I'll be happy when I pay off my student loans'; 'I'll be happy when I graduate and get my dream job.' These are not quotes from one particular person, but a belief that a lot of us hold. Essentially, we're all playing a giant waiting game, and it needs to stop.

Life satisfaction – or better yet, happiness – isn't something you wait for.

Frankly, if you're not happy now, well, you may never be. The reason for this is, as we achieve more success, we're happy for a period of time, but because our desires rise simultaneously with our success, we revert back to that base level of happiness. The result is never feeling satisfied or happier. We see this with children – when they get a new toy, they're entertained for a few days and then they revert to their happiness set point, and dream of the next toy that comes their way.

There's evidence for why our brain operates this way. Most of us possess something called the optimistic bias, which is the tendency to think that our future will be better than our present.[3] But I refuse to believe that these 'set points' and 'biases' are permanent. In my opinion, this is why mindset work is absolutely crucial when it comes to happiness as well as success. We have to learn how to bring ourselves back to the present moment – to find satisfaction here and now instead of continuously kicking that can.

So, what would that look like for you? Starting a gratitude journal? Being present for a conversation with your husband? Doing something you love today versus 'when you have time'? One of the easiest ways to make this shift is to go back to the basics.

Go Back to the Basics

One fascinating thing that tends to happen with my clients (and me) is that we forget what got us to this place or level of success. For example, in the beginning of our IHML programs (just like in this book), we're very focused on mindset, before we get to the how-tos and strategy. For weeks, my clients are reading regularly, journaling, practicing gratitude, monitoring their thoughts and celebrating wins big and small. And they start to see big shifts in their levels of happiness and life satisfaction.

But then, as they move on to the next stage of building their business and going for their dreams, they forget the basics. Their time is taken over by funnels, emails, sales calls. That's great, and it needs to happen, but we have to remember what's helped us get to this place and what was working until we stopped doing it. It's like a person with depression saying they don't need their happiness pills anymore because they're 'better' – but the pills are what contributed to them feeling better! Make sense?

In many ways, I'd forgotten the basics in my own life. My mindset work, meditation, journaling, gratitude practice – I'd convinced myself that I didn't need it and that the answer was to work harder. Three years into my business, I'd gained 35 pounds. My self-care game clearly wasn't much to write home about. I took care of my clients but most of the time I forgot myself. I made sure my clients celebrated, but did I?

I soon realized I had to focus on the daily habits that would create my happiness. Ultimately, I had to give myself permission to go back to the basics and pay attention to what actually made me happy and made me feel good.

Stop Pushing

The movie *Bad Moms* is completely bonkers and hilarious. If you haven't seen it, it's the story of a mom, played by Mila Kunis, and her quest to get over this idea of perfection. She's barely holding it together, with two young children and a husband who is pretty much her third child, a job that's supposed to be part-time yet she works harder than anyone there, and pressure from the PTA Nazi, played by Christina Applegate. Throughout her crisis, she bands together with two other moms, played by Kristen Bell and Kathryn Hahn.

In one of the early scenes, the ladies are describing their ultimate mom fantasies over drinks and Kristen's character surprises them all with her admission. She reveals that sometimes, she wishes she could be involved in a car accident and be a little bit injured. Nothing too bad – just enough so that she could be admitted to hospital for two weeks (all covered by insurance of course) and have other people take care of her instead of her needing to take care of everyone else.

Although I'm not a mom, and I wouldn't call them fantasies, I had the same feeling about my business at one point. One of my darkest moments was when I realized I was actually hoping to get sick because then I wouldn't have to keep working. How did I get to this point, I wondered.

Drop the Addiction to Hard Work

One of the tendencies I uncovered in myself (that was definitely a happiness blocker) was an addiction to hard work. It was like I was birthing this new life, but stuck in a never-ending cycle of labor, after labor, after labor. Constant pushing.

Now you may be saying to yourself, well, there's nothing wrong with a little hard work, and in some ways, you're right. There are times when hard work is a positive – there are times when the fact that I'm never satisfied drives me forward; but there are also times when both of those negatively affect my health, happiness, and relationships (and leave me wanting to get sick). It's the same for you, so you have to start to recognize when you're using your powers for good and when those tendencies are harmful to you and your dreams.

I love what Steve Siebold has to say on this subject: 'If hard work was the secret to financial success, every construction worker and cocktail waitress would be rich.'[4] In other words, there's more to making money than plain old hard work, or even luck.

I grew up with a father who woke at 4 a.m. to go to work, every day of his life. He had a heart attack in his early 40s. I've no idea if those two things are related, but I do know that what was modeled for me was a 14-hour work day. I figured that was just the reality of running a business and being successful, so I too was a card-carrying member of the Hard Work Club.

But as I moved forward in my business, I secretly hoped there was another way. Yes, you have to show up. Yes, you have to take massive action on behalf of your dreams, but did I really want to kill myself in the process of getting where I wanted to go? Did it have to be this hard? And if that was what was required, was I really willing to do it?

The sad truth is that many of us are willing to do anything – even if it means putting our health and relationships on the line. It's hard to see another way. When we think about not working hard, we wrestle with the fear that changing our habits will mean the loss of the success we've created. I often wondered what would happen if I wasn't online in the middle of the night, answering emails. What would happen if I didn't take the call. What would happen if I said 'no' to the interview.

Many of us fall for the lure of hard work. It allows us to feel in control.

After all, hard work provides some sort of peace when you think about it: working hard = success. It's a tried-and-tested equation. It allows us to feel in control of our current and future reality. Don't get me wrong, hard work is one of the reasons I'm here today writing this book. But when I uncovered the fact that I literally hoped I'd get sick so I could have an excuse not to work, it was obvious that some part of me felt there was no way out. Maybe that was a normal reality for some people, but I didn't want that to be my normal. Plus, I knew that working that way wasn't sustainable. I wanted to play the long game, not run my business for a few years and then quit.

I've consulted with plenty of clients who share my habit of overworking. They come to me stressed, unhealthy, in tears nearly every session. It's like they're on a hamster wheel and they don't know how to get off. Because this is an addiction – no different to an addiction to eating too much sugar or obsessively checking Facebook – it takes some retraining of the mind to understand that it's not a recipe for success. We need to reinvent the definition of hard work and add rest into the equation.

But here's where this becomes tricky for women like us – once we've seen the result of hard work (and believe me, it's all around us), it's difficult to believe there's another way. I had to retrain my mind to believe that I could have everything I desired, even if I worked less. And in fact, if I continued to work in the way I had been, everything I desired *wasn't* going to become my reality.

Necessity

One of the ways I was able to retrain my mind was by focusing on necessity. Brendon Burchard defines necessity as 'the emotional drive that makes great performance a must instead of a preference.'[5] I wasn't prepared to lower my goals, so I had to focus on the result I wanted that operating in this new way would bring (or I hoped it would bring). Another way to think of this is the ROI (return on investment).

For example, my ROI always has to do with money and success. That's just the reality. Through years of experience, I knew what hard work would get me, but I didn't know what self-love and joy would get me. I had to trust my coaches to share their own experience with me and guide me. And from what they told me, self-love was the answer to everything I desired! (I remember our relationship coach telling me that I'd make more money if I had more sex and pleasure in my life. She knew how to appeal to me!)

I had to think about the ROI of rest, the ROI of stretching, the ROI of turning my phone off at 7 p.m. in order to connect with what it was going to do for me (and how much more money I was going to make). I had to pair the two together. Self-love = more money. Rest = more money. Pleasure = more money.

It's imperative that you find *your* necessity too and connect to the desired result. So is it freedom? Time? Health? Money? You get to decide, and by the way, there isn't a right or wrong answer. It's whatever resonates with you.

Success Tip

Take time to ponder those questions above and uncover your own ROI before moving forward with this chapter.

Think of Yourself as an Athlete

One of the other concepts that helped me make a huge shift and dial back my addiction to hard work and constant pushing was starting to think of myself as an athlete. (Stick with me.) Throughout this book, we've uncovered the fact that you know you're meant for something big, and in order to achieve something big, you have to show up differently; and it does take a lot of physical output and time to reach your goals. An athlete training for a big game or sporting event adheres to certain practices and ways of life that the rest of us don't (and probably wouldn't think about).

Now, rest assured that I'm not talking about taking ice baths or completely giving up coffee, but I am suggesting that you look at yourself differently from now on. You are not normal, and so the action you take cannot be normal. What you put in your body cannot be normal. The decisions you make cannot be normal. There's nothing normal about wanting to change the world and do something big.

Think about it like this – what would an athlete training for the Olympics eat? How much water would they drink? How many hours of sleep would they get? What boundaries would they put in place? How would they spend their time?

Your dreams are about longevity, right? You don't want to be a one-hit-wonder. You don't want to peak and then crash and burn. For that reason, you have to think about achieving success as a marathon, not a sprint. And you have to ask yourself, what is it going to take to consistently show up and take action on behalf of your dreams? (The key word here being *consistently*.)

Time to Recover

There's been plenty of research conducted on what recovery does for athletes – in fact, recovery is *essential* to their success. As my husband James says: 'Your ability to create something as big as your ever-expanding goals is dependent on your ability to maintain and sustain momentum for the long term. When we're working, learning, creating, exercising, we are stressing our minds and our bodies, which promotes growth. But remember, growth only happens in recovery. We must meet the stressors of our mind and body with an equal amount of recovery in order to grow.'

In my mind, it helps to think about adding in *downtime* to work – time for fun, rest, moments of silence – rather than focusing on no longer working hard. After all, like I said, you really need both. When I'm in flow and in my Zone of Genius, I can get more done in a day that most people accomplish in a week or two. But there I go again: wearing hard work like a badge of honor. You see, I too am still a work in progress.

Protect Your Sleep

Ever since college, when my roommate stayed up until the early hours of the morning listening to opera music and studying, I've had issues with sleep. While I was building my business, I experienced many restless nights when I'd wake up at 3 a.m. for what appeared to be no reason at all.

One day, I posted a question in a group I belong to with fellow seven-figure (and even eight- and nine-figure) companies and my own high-level coach. I asked the members to share the one thing that moved the needle the most for them in terms of energy and reducing stress. Most people listed out multiple practices and shifts, but there was one that all of them had in common: sleep. In particular, one person said they learned to 'protect their sleep.' I'd never thought about it that way – protecting my sleep.

I'm guilty of looking at my phone late into the night – even email sometimes. With the majority of our clients and team in the US, it seems like we're always 'on.' I knew this couldn't continue forever, and frankly it didn't need to. I'd heard Robin Sharma say, 'Your phone is costing you your fortune,'[6] and at the time, I thought that was a little dramatic. But maybe he was right?

(In case you're unaware of it, the light emitted by your phone puts your brain into 'awake' mode. So when you look at it right before bedtime, it stops your brain from producing the melatonin that's required to induce sleep. Watching TV does the same thing.)

Although it's still a work in progress for me, I've learned to protect my sleep, and that includes not using my phone late at night, lighting lavender candles, taking a bath or shower before bed, not drinking coffee past noon, and ending my work day around 6:30 p.m. It's important to figure out what works for you and start protecting your sleep like your life depends on it (because it does). So if sleep isn't at the top of your list of important things, it needs to be – starting today.

Massage and Self-Care

Another key component to my success has been self-care. For me, that comes in the form of regular massages (I'll get one every week most of the time, and then have spa days pretty much every quarter). I also do simple things like buy myself flowers, light beautiful candles around the house that inspire me, spray my bed with lavender spray at night, get my nails done regularly, and take long showers. There's no right way to practice self-care, so you need to start paying attention to what makes you feel good and do more of that. It's that simple.

Create Boundaries Not Barriers

In addition to focusing on myself, I had to start paying attention to my interactions with others and learn to make friends with boundaries.

Did you know that boundaries are actually a form of self-love and happiness? I love how Danielle LaPorte describes this and differentiates boundaries from barriers. She says, 'Boundaries are like a fence with a gate – the energy can come and go. Barriers are like a shield that you drag around – ready to defend yourself from attacks.'[7]

I had to learn to protect myself in a way that worked for me. I had to pay attention to the people I allowed into my life, as well as the quality of my thoughts, and boundaries are just that – quality control.

I realized that allowing people in who didn't get my mission and didn't show kindness toward me – or even allowing clients to overstep – was a form of self-abuse. That may sound extreme to you, but it's really not. Any time we put others first and deny what we really want, and what's good for us, we're not showing ourselves love, appreciation, and respect. We have to teach people what's acceptable and what falls into alignment with what we desire, not just tolerate things. I don't even want 'tolerate' to be a part of your vocabulary. It doesn't have to be. Envision your ideal life and create it – boundaries and all.

Stop Saying Yes When You Mean No

One of the easiest ways to think about boundaries is to focus on what you're saying 'yes' to in your life. For example, saying 'yes' when you actually mean 'no' is the opposite of self-love. You're essentially putting someone else's needs and desires before your own, so how could that possibly be a positive?

You and I both know that this doesn't result in anything good – even if the intention is to make someone else happy – because you end up resenting the other person and feel out of alignment. (Plus, although you think you're being stealthy, people can tell when you're not being truthful and it does nothing for the relationship but breed mistrust.)

When I finally got this concept and started to really pay attention to my 'yeses,' I was shocked. How often throughout my day was I putting others before myself? Yes, I want to be loving, generous, and kind-hearted, but did that really mean I had to come in last in the order of important people?

Let's get one thing straight: putting yourself first doesn't mean you're selfish.

Putting yourself first means that you know what's required for you to show up as your best self, to perform at your highest level, to be your happiest, to be able to give to others because your glass is full. And clearly it means that other people benefit from being around you because you're happier and in alignment.

It means your relationships are pure and meaningful because you've chosen them carefully, and you're not trying to squeeze in time with people – you've deliberately created time. How incredible would it feel to have relationships like that? It's possible, and it starts by you saying yes only when you want to say yes. (And if you want to put a label on it, let's call it self-*full*.)

In her book *What I Know For Sure*, Oprah Winfrey talks about the first time she declined to donate money. The request had come from Stevie Wonder, no less, but she was so over writing checks that she didn't want to write and couldn't bear to do it any longer. She was so nervous to have the conversation with him, but when she told him her truth, he responded like it was no big deal. For her, it was everything.[8]

Why does it take so many of us so long? Why are we constantly sweeping what we want under the rug? Why are we putting the needs of our husbands, kids, clients, and employees before our own? Want a one-word answer? Fear.

One of the main reasons we don't put ourselves first is the fear of what people will think and what will happen if we show up differently. It goes back to the evolutionary example I gave earlier: we don't want to be disliked. And we, as women especially, don't want people to think we're a bitch. We don't want people to question the 'goodness' of our character.

And of course we want to be kind; of course we want to have friends – but you're telling me you're willing to put yourself last in the process? It needs to stop, and it starts with saying yes only when you mean yes, and putting an end to being a bitch to yourself.

Stop Making the Present Moment Wrong

Another key component of my personal transformation has been time. In the first quarter of 2017, I completed an exercise about time. I took a few minutes to think about that day's date and then wrote down the first thoughts that came to mind about it. (I highly recommend you try this yourself and see what comes up.) Here's what came out on paper:

- I can't believe how quickly this year is going by.

- I have trips and events coming up this month – that makes me super excited, but I also feel like I have a million things to do beforehand.

- We have two launches right around the corner – are we ready?! (Again, overwhelm sets in.)

- How is it already 2017, and how am I 31 years old?

- I can't believe I've lived in London for nearly seven years. (Have I made the most of it?!

- I can't believe I've been running my business for nearly three years. (In some ways it feels like I've done more in three years than I ever thought I would, but at the same time, it feels like it's gone by quickly.)

I remember writing that and immediately feeling like I wasn't far enough along. Realizing I was 'behind' on my daily tasks. There are a lot of things that come up when we think about time and timing, right? The truth about time and me is that we haven't always been friends, and we're still a work in progress.

I've often thought I should be further along; thought I did something wrong to end up in this place; felt like I was running out of time; felt overwhelmed about everything on my plate. And one of my more recent (and biggest) realizations about time is that I often made the present moment wrong. That last one is a doozy.

How often do you make the present moment wrong? If you're thinking anything like the thoughts in that list, you're making the present moment wrong. The issue with this is that when we're so focused on what's not happening or the ways in which we're behind, we get more of those feelings, and we stall.

Especially when you're just starting out, it's essential you see that everything is happening as it's meant to.

Even those challenges are helping you. You have to become the person you're required to be, in order to get there. What if that challenge is helping you do that? What if without it, you'll stay in the same place? What if times are challenging right now for a reason? (We'll cover that in the next chapter.)

What if you aren't meant to know the answer yet? What if you're on the cusp? Remember, there's so much going on beneath the surface that doesn't meet the eye. Everything is happening exactly as it's meant to. You are and always have been in the right place at the right time.

Shift Anxiety

Making peace with time had an unexpected side effect for me; reduced anxiety. When I was first building I Heart My Life, I suffered from anxiety in the evenings. In fact, most nights I was anxious. I asked James to place his hands on the top of my chest. Sometimes it comforted me, and sometimes it made me cry harder.

Now the way I deal with anxiety is to focus on my mindset and get clear on the thoughts and words that are going through my mind at the moment the anxiety is present. Yes, there are times when anxiety can serve us – maybe there really is something you need to pay attention to or a red flag that you previously missed. Only you can discern what your anxiety means.

For me, most of the time it means I'm living in the future: my mind wants to go into fortune-teller mode and predict the outcome of something. And most of the time, it's not pretty. In those moments, I remember that I need all my energy to make things happen, and right now, I'm wasting it on the worry. It truly is a waste; I hope you can see that.

This reminder of leaking energy helps me shift my anxiety because I remember how much I want to do in this one life. I need that full bucket of energy and I cannot afford to waste it on anything other than living the life I want and having an impact. Plus, as we previously covered, most of our worries never actually happen. More importantly, even if they did, I know I'm strong enough to be able to handle them.

Follow Your Fear

One of the tools I recommend you implement when anxiety comes up is following your fear. Say you're anxious about a client not paying on time. Follow that fear. What would happen if they didn't pay on time? What would happen if they pulled out of the contract? Run through the scenario in your mind and even make a plan for if that happened. Once you do that, you'll start to see that your worries aren't actually that scary, and if they ever did come to life, you'd be okay.

Be Kind to You

How often do you feel pressure? Pressure to achieve, do, or be something? Pressure runs rampant in our everyday life. One of the concepts I had to come to terms with is that pressure doesn't actually exist. Well, it does, but it's all self-imposed.

While at a retreat with my coach, I asked her why she thought I was so hard on others – especially my team. She simply said, 'Because you're hard on yourself.' I was speechless. That was a wake-up call I needed.

The reality is, if you're putting pressure and being hard on yourself, the chances are you're making things more difficult than they're meant to be. When there's no room for error, life isn't fun and you don't have all the energy you need to achieve your big dreams. Pressure is draining. Releasing the pressure and recognizing that most people are doing the best they can (yourself included) is incredibly transformational.

Have Foresight

As you're shifting into the world of self-love, it's important to identify what might throw you off track. For example, if you were looking to eat more healthily, you would do your best not to purchase all the sugary stuff. You'd surround yourself with healthy food so the temptation was lower. You wouldn't go to the café with all the croissants and cookies because it would be too easy to give in.

It's the same with your dreams. So much of becoming more successful is about you being self-aware and honest with yourself about your natural tendencies. Don't make them wrong or judge them, but recognize your patterns and make decisions that set you up for success.

On my own journey, I realized that, to a certain extent, Facebook was ruining my life. (I know, more dramatics.) I knew it wasn't all of Facebook, but one day I found myself down the Facebook rabbit hole looking at a little girl's 4th birthday party photo album – I didn't even know the mother! And then I saw that someone's 90-something dad had renewed his driver's license, and then the next photo was of someone's trip to Italy (again – I didn't know this person).

It wasn't that those posts evoked negative emotions in me, but I had to be real – this time I was spending scrolling was taking me away from my purpose. Maybe even costing me my fortune and impact. So I spent an hour unfollowing people on Facebook. If I didn't know them, didn't have a relationship with them, didn't like what they stood for, didn't feel that their posts added value to my life, I unfriended them. I also blocked any ads I didn't need or want to see anymore. That's just one simple example, but sometimes the simple things that can have the most impact.

Trust Yourself

When I think about the personal transformation I went through in my quest for self-love and happiness, it comes down to trust. I had to learn to trust myself above all else. Trust that when I was tired, I rested; trust that when I felt sad, I cried; trust that when something didn't feel right, it was a no. I had to trust that I was enough and deserving, and soon, I started to see huge shifts. I was happier, less anxious, clearer, and overall more energetic. I worried less about what people thought of me, and learned to make what *I* thought about me my main concern.

We're going to continue to talk about trust throughout the rest of the book, but just envision what trusting not only yourself, but life and others, would do for your level of happiness.

A Final Note

Ultimately, I've discovered that the quest for self-love and happiness is a lifelong journey. I have good days and bad days, and you will too. But I'm so excited to see how self-love changes your life. Because believe me, it has the power to change *everything*.

Action Step

What does putting yourself first look like in your own life? How would self-love change your life and level of happiness? What do you think would make you happier?

This is a very personal chapter, and it will apply to your life in a unique way. For that reason, go back through each section and choose at least one way you can implement these practices, starting this week. Pay attention to which of the concepts really speaks to you and start there.

CHAPTER 9

Challenge

'Every adversity has a seed of either equal or greater value or benefit.'[1]

NAPOLEON HILL

I used to think that having a positive mindset meant that nothing negative would ever happen to me. We'd continue to go up, and up, and up in our business and life. (Yes, that was wishful thinking.) I didn't want to join the realists. After all, I was used to challenge during my quarter-life crisis; I'd been there and done that. But as my reality changed and my business grew, I didn't expect challenge to be there in the car with me along the journey. Let's just say, I was wrong…

In July 2017, while in New York City for a publicity retreat I was attending, I opened my computer and pulled up my email inbox to check my messages. I spotted an email from one of the clients in my high-level mastermind (it caught my attention because she wasn't someone who usually emailed me). I opened it quickly and my heart sank. It said, 'I'd like to withdraw my place in the mastermind.'

I texted James to ask him if he'd seen the email – he hadn't. We were both stunned. A few hours later, we received two more emails, just like it. I was so upset that I didn't go to the retreat that day. I spoke to one of our coaches, to try to get some personal support and a game plan in place for getting to the root of what was happening with our clients. I'd never dealt with anything like that before, so I didn't know what to do.

During that time in my life, I had a tendency to take things personally. I've always been emotional, and it's difficult for me to separate that emotion from my business. After all, the word 'heart' is an integral part of the work that I do – I lead with my heart, I make heart-based decisions, and I let my clients into my heart.

The next day, I was supposed to be at day 3 of the event in New York City, and then fly to Italy to meet James in Florence. I ended up calling the airline and switching my flight to that evening. I wanted to be out of the city and with James so we could try to figure this out together. I got on a 4:30 p.m. flight and by the time I arrived in Florence, we had two more emails from clients wanting to leave the mastermind.

We'd been looking forward to this trip all year, as it was our first real time off in a while. 'Why did this have to happen now?' I wondered. During our time away, two more emails came in, making a total of seven.

For confidentiality reasons, I'm not going to go into the details of this experience, except to say it resulted in a large financial loss for our company, and it was one of the most difficult challenges of my life thus far. When you throw everything you have into your work and want so badly to create a positive experience and massive change for your clients, when something like that happens, it's like a giant slap in the face. But in so many ways, like most challenges as you'll come to learn, it's the best thing that could have happened.

Why Challenge Is Important

The truth is that I don't actually like admitting to my challenge. I'd much rather not have anything like this to share. But I do: I'm human, and I'm always learning. And I ultimately know that challenge presents itself for my benefit.

During my moments of challenge, I've often reminded myself that challenge is good. I remember that strong muscles are a result of microscopic tears in the muscles which, once repaired, lead to increased strength.[2] So that's what challenge is for us too – tearing and then becoming stronger.

Challenge creates strength and allows you to grow in ways that positive experiences, well, can't. It's also one of those great teachers which, when we're open to it and allow it in, can transform us in unimaginable ways. Think about it like this – when you go to that workout class, you know the teacher's support and drive will help you work 10 times harder than you'd choose to do on your own. And for that reason, you get stronger and see more results in a shorter amount of time. It's the same thing with challenge: it's making us stronger, yet the majority of us want to avoid it at all costs.

In her book *Trust*, Iyanla Vanzant says, 'While you want to be saved from the fall off the cliff, the law wants you to realize how long you can hang on, building your muscles in the process.'[3] Isn't that a beautiful way of thinking about it? I like to think about the Universe arranging events specifically for me, for my benefit, and that includes challenge. It makes me stronger and gives me more gifts than success ever will.

And I know that challenge is never just about me. I heard Elizabeth Gilbert speak at Oprah's live event in 2014, and she said she was so nervous before her appearance, until she realized it wasn't actually about her. There were people who needed to hear her message; it was about them.

I believe my challenge is not only for my growth, but for yours as well. When you hear about my challenge and experience your own – which you will, because we're all humans with challenges – I don't want you to feel alone. I want you to know that it's normal. The more we share our ups and downs, the better off we'll all be. You'll know that if something doesn't go as planned, you aren't a failure. And all that matters is what you do next.

I know it's not always easy, but the sooner you learn to turn challenge into a positive, the quicker you'll be able to move through it and develop respect for it – and of course, experience its lessons and benefits. In order to do that, you have to flip the switch on your thinking about challenge. Let's look at a few ways to do that together.

Celebration Break

How would it feel to celebrate all your past challenges and the challenges to come? Give it a shot now!

Challenge Is Preparation

I see challenge as preparation. None of us are born knowing everything we need to know about creating success. It requires growth and learning, and I believe the fast path to that growth and learning is challenge. Think about it like this: when you're young and you fall off your bike and hit your head, you learn really quickly that you need to wear a helmet, much quicker than if you see someone else fall or if your parents just tell you it's going to hurt, if or when that happens.

Similarly, my sister is almost six feet tall, and during her pre-teen years, there were periods when she grew at lightning speed. Her legs would hurt during these growth spurts, and there were days when she'd throw herself on the bed and cry. Although it was difficult to witness that, my family and I couldn't do anything about it. It had to happen. And it's the same for you in your own time of challenge. It's on behalf of your own growth and development. It's a good thing!

The challenge I experienced with our clients leaving the mastermind forced me to become the next-level version of me. We had to get our finances together, and that led to some amazing personal and business growth – it definitely resulted in strength I didn't know I had.

For most of us, the difficulty of challenge isn't hindsight; we can look back and see why something happened and how we were able to grow from it. The test is to see those positives *while you're in the midst of it*. But it is possible. You can see the silver lining if you're willing to look for it. And even if you can't see it, you can use your past as an example. I'm sure there have been plenty of challenges you've already experienced that ended up being blessings in disguise.

What if you treated the current challenge exactly the same way, and assumed it too was a blessing? Most of us have had enough experience with challenge to be able to guess at what the benefits of a current situation may be, and the sooner you start looking for those blessings, the sooner they'll appear. It's when we resist challenge that it persists longer than necessary.

Success Tip

Think of one previous challenge that resulted in a positive outcome. Have that challenge to hand to use as an example during difficult times that arise in the future.

Stop Playing the Victim

The topic of victim mentality could be a whole book in itself. Victim tendencies run rampant in women, and I see this all the time in the work that I do with driven entrepreneurs. Victims are people who blame the world for anything that happens to them. They take no personal responsibility for challenges or hardships. They feel that everyone is out to get them, and for that reason, they often go into blame mode during difficult moments.

If that resonates with you, I want you to listen closely and hear me when I say: You are responsible for everything that happens in your life. Now before you throw this book out the window, stick with me. If you believe that your thoughts, words, and actions create your reality, then that means the positive as well as the negative!

You can't have one without the other – that wouldn't work. This isn't a selective process – it's universal. So if you're bringing about the good, you're also bringing about the bad. It's no one's fault but your own. (Please hear me when I say that I'm not talking about things like physical or sexual abuse; I'm referring to instances like the story I shared at the beginning of this chapter.)

For example, when our clients asked to leave our program, I had to take a look at which element of that I was responsible for. What could I have done better? And in what ways did I actually manifest that experience? Of course I hated the fact that I'd manifested the experience at all, and every ounce of me wanted to deny that reality – I'm human and I want to feel good, and believe me, nothing about this felt good. But I had to force myself to take a vulnerable look in the mirror. Although it's rarely easy, you have to take responsibility for your reality and remember it's happening for you, not to you.

I know that's potentially a difficult concept to stomach, but it's a crucial one to integrate and understand. Look at it like this – if you know your tendency is to blame others when bad things happen, it's your job to stick with the challenge instead, because only then will you truly get the lesson.

Think about challenge as a gift – if you just pass it on to someone else and don't actually open it, look at it, or even acknowledge it, you're missing the whole point! Ask yourself, what's the lesson? How is this meant to stretch you to the next level? How is this helping you drop blame and take personal responsibility?

Challenge can also reveal limiting beliefs. Going back to my experience, I believe one of the reasons why the mastermind scenario played out was because I had a deep-seated fear of losing my business. Entrepreneurs in my family had lost businesses and I was recreating the pattern in my family. And if it wasn't for some savvy financial planning and support, that could have happened. Luckily, through my challenge I learned my own strength and resilience and was able to shift that fear. The same is possible for you.

Use Challenge as a Sign of Growth

What if the bigger the challenge, the bigger the gift? That's how I choose to view challenge. I love the quote at the beginning of this chapter by Napoleon Hill, from his book *Grow Rich! With Peace of Mind*: 'Every adversity has a seed of either equal or greater value or benefit.'[4]

To me, those words are a reminder that it's so important to have faith and keep moving forward, no matter what, because the most difficult moments are setting you up for growth. You may not see it just yet, but on the other side of the struggle there's something even greater about to sprout up – huge breakthroughs, major lessons, massive clarity: all right beneath the ground. The bigger the challenge, the greater the profit.

Challenge helps you identify where you can grow as a person – it's essential to your success.

So, no matter where you're at in your life at this present moment – whether you're more of the 'hot mess' that I was or on your way to your dreams – when challenges come up and things feel less than stellar, you have to remember that they're happening for a reason. As Robin Sharma says, 'All change is hard at first, messy in the middle, and beautiful at the end.'[5] The messier that middle, the more beautiful at the end, so stop making the present moment wrong. It has a purpose!

One of the other helpful ways I've learned to deal with challenge is through comparing it to the change of seasons. If you think about it, it makes total sense: spring is bountiful and summer is lush, but throughout all that time, the planet is also preparing for fall and winter, when things literally die. As Iyanla Vanzant says: 'Each season supports a purpose that advances life.'[6] It's the same with your life and success.

Our challenges are necessary, and frankly, we shouldn't be that surprised when they occur. The planet doesn't question when the leaves fall or when animals go into hibernation. That's part of the experience of life! When you're going through a challenging time, look at it as a season in your life. You're being prepared for something – something new is on its way, there's about to be a rebirth, a seed has been planted. Find a metaphor that resonates and speaks to you.

I get really excited when my clients are experiencing challenge. For example, one of my clients messaged me saying that she'd just booked a trip to her vacation home to work on the creation of her new course in peace. She said as she purchased the ticket for the flight, she had heart palpitations because it was the first time she was going to be away from her four kids. I couldn't have been more proud than I was in that moment. That challenge and step was transformation right before my eyes.

The same thing happens when my clients 'unexpectedly' lose their job or their fiancé leaves them – I know something juicy is about to happen, and that they're actually being prepped internally for something bigger; space is being created for that 'greatness' or a shift to come in.

You're not meant to be great overnight, and that's not how this works. You have to *become* great. There's no such thing as an instant success story. (And sometimes those who do experience faster success discover it actually doesn't serve them because they weren't ready. There's a reason why young celebrities get into trouble and make a mess of their life – they don't know who they really are, what they want, or how to be the person with their level of success.) Challenge grooms you for everything you desire. Challenge isn't the enemy – it's your teacher, bodybuilder, and coach rolled into one.

Challenge isn't the enemy – it's your teacher, bodybuilder, and coach rolled into one.

Shift Your Focus

The good news is that in those moments of despair, there's always something that is working simultaneously. Remember, the Law of Polarity dictates that you can't have something that doesn't work without also having something that does work at the same time. And you can't have the good without the bad, so of course the bad exists!

One of the very best parts of going after my dreams and running my own business has been the incredible clients who've trusted me to help guide them on their own journeys. For every woman who complains (and believe me, I've gotten some nasty messages), there are 15 women who have an amazing experience. But we all know that, for some reason, that one complainer stands out more than the rest. However, you can choose to focus on the positive instead of the negative. You can flip the switch!

For example, in those moments when I get the scathing email or Facebook message or mean comment on a video, I focus on the clients who have brought me tears of joy as I watch them overcome obstacles and reach their goals. Every client is a reminder that my big dreams truly were meant for me – that putting myself and my gifts out there to the world, despite the struggles and fears that come with entrepreneurship, has been totally worth it.

Challenge Is Normal

In case you're unaware, challenge is normal. And I know, I know, you're not looking to be normal, but what I mean is that everyone who has done something great has experienced challenge. That's why Brendon Burchard has such a famous saying like 'honor the struggle.' The struggle can be real for those of us who choose to follow our heart. Those who came before you experienced the same thing. Honor them. Know that they paved the way for you in many ways. And trust that just like them, you too will make it to the other side and be stronger for it.

Be Grateful for the Mountain

One more thing – it's imperative to practice gratitude through the fear, sorrow and pain you experience. As Oprah Winfrey once said, 'I got so focused on the difficulty of the climb that I lost sight of being grateful for simply having a mountain to climb.'[7]

Challenge is a gift. And the other gift is that you're alive and feeling it. I want you to really understand the level of gratitude I possess for all the challenges I've been through over the past few years. Here are just some of the ways in which they changed me…

- I stopped caring (as much) about what people think, and I stopped worrying.
- I was able to reduce my anxiety levels.
- I learned about my own strength and that I could handle anything.
- I released generations of harmful patterns.

- I became more confident and was able to speak my truth, which created more honest relationships and conversations in my life.
- I became stronger as a leader.
- I got clear on what I really wanted and was willing to fight for.
- I connected with those people in my life who really cared about me, and learned who my real friends actually are. People came out of the woodwork to support us and that fostered a much deeper connection.
- I developed a deeper gratitude for money.

Stay on the mountain. Keep climbing. The view is imminent, and it's breathtaking. You've got this.

Action Step

How has challenge transformed your life? Write a list like the one under 'Be Grateful for the Mountain,' and the next time challenge arises, use the tools in this chapter to help you move through it and see its benefits.

CHAPTER 10

Support

'Show me your friends and I'll predict your fortune.'[1]

ROBIN SHARMA

In November 2017, I was approached by a contact James had made at a mastermind who said she wanted to talk to me about being on a radio show and also having my own show.

James and I got on the phone with her and as she described the opportunity – my own radio show that would also be featured on iHeartRadio and other top networks – I felt myself clam up. I already had so much on my plate and there was no way I could add something else to it. So I told her 'no.'

It felt horrible, declining something that, from the outside looking in, was so much of what I'd always wanted. I couldn't quite put my finger on it, but as I already had a habit of wanting to do all the stuff, it felt empowering to decline something for once.

However, a few weeks later – during a spinning class – I had a breakthrough. If you had seen me on the bike that day, you would have thought I was having a breakdown. There were tons of tears and I was riding like a crazy woman (I got a personal best score that class). But it was really an incredible moment.

As John Legend played in the background, I had a vision of James sitting on the porch of a beautiful home in Hawaii. (If you've seen a photo of Oprah's home in Maui, it looked like that.) I was in another room, peering around the corner; looking outside at him. He was talking to a close friend of ours. I couldn't see their face, but it was someone whom we both trust and love – this was obvious by the feeling I had as I listened to their conversation.

In the vision, James told our friend that he couldn't believe how different our life was now, compared to where we started. He described how hard it was, but that it was worth all the effort. And in my vision, I had an innate knowing that my show – the I Heart My Life Show (IHML Show) – was part of what had gotten us there. It was glaringly obvious; although it scared me, I had to do this.

So I got in touch with the contact and we launched the IHML Show on January 1, 2018.

Your Network Is Your Net Worth

In 2017, when James and I experienced our business challenges, it was the support system in our lives that made all the difference. We didn't talk about this with our family members – it was the new entrepreneurial community that we leaned on. The coaches I hired for self-love? They were there for us every step of the way.

My friends from group programs – they got it and some had even experienced the same thing themselves. We also hired someone to take a deeper look into our financials. He was a lifesaver in many ways.

I'd never been so grateful for the people in my life, and for the first time, so much of my fear of the future began to fade away. I knew that with the network I'd created, I was safe. I could make it through anything. It also brought James and me closer together. We became a team. We realized that we were so much more powerful together.

I didn't start my business with the intention of making friends all around the world – as an introvert I've always been happy in my own company, behind my computer – but 2017 taught me the importance of connection.

It also taught me that it's okay for friendships to change or even fade away. Are we really meant to be friends with everyone for a lifetime? No. And that's especially the case when we're on a growth-based trajectory in which we're personally changing and transforming at a rapid pace.

This chapter is about the various components of support – building relationships as well as letting them go, and about the importance of support in helping you create the success you desire.

Why Our Relationships Matter

Before we go any further, I want you to understand why your social circle is a critical part of your success. First, let's take an inventory of the people with whom you spend the most time throughout your week. (Pick a standard week in your life from which to pull this data.) They may be friends or family members, but for those who spend 40+ hours in an office, they may be colleagues.

Regardless of your particular scenario, ask yourself what *kind* of people are on your list. Are they driven? Do they want what you want? Are they supportive? Or are they Debbie Downers who connect over strife and negativity, and thrive on gossip and seeing other people fail?

Although most of us like to think we aren't easily swayed by others' behavior, studies show that in fact we are; our behavior is a combination of the behavior of people with whom we spend most time. Researchers have even found that the people you sit next to in a restaurant dictate how much you eat! It's true: you mimic the eating habits of those who surround you, even if they're strangers. You'll eat more, order the dessert, have another glass of wine etc. Others' influence over our food choices is even greater if they're people we know, like, and trust, as we feel a stronger need to identify with them. We use others' eating behavior as a guide for our own.[2]

I've observed this in my own life, with exercise; although I'm not an avid yogi and getting out of bed to work out at 6:30 a.m. doesn't always feel so great, once I'm in the studio surrounded by other people who have also made the effort and decided not to hit that snooze button, it changes everything. The difference that the energy of the people around us makes is truly amazing – not only when it comes to fitness, but in life and business too.

I know that when I'm surrounded by people who are on a mission, it takes my own performance and drive to another level; and when I'm surrounded by those Debbie Downers, I feel it too. It's the same with your success, and this is why what we're covering in this chapter is essential to you reaching new heights in your life.

Trust me, I know firsthand how difficult it can be when you're trying to chart your own path while surrounded by people who don't really 'get' you. Not everyone is cut out to go against the grain, and those who aren't often don't understand why someone would want to take the big risk of pursuing what appears to be a wild and crazy, pie-in-the-sky sort of dream. It can be a lonely journey. As a coach of female entrepreneurs and driven women, I see the challenges that they face when they don't have support from family, friends, or their spouse; or even worse, are ridiculed for taking steps toward their vision.

Perhaps, as you ponder the possibility of going after your dreams, you're facing some naysayers in your life? Maybe your friends mean well, but they just can't get on board with your 'risky' goals. If so, I want you to know that you're not alone.

Handling Those Who Don't 'Get' You

For example, throughout my journey, I've had experiences of friends and family being supportive, and also the opposite. For instance, I traveled to Ohio to visit my family for Christmas in December 2015. I was proud of what I'd achieved thus far – about to hit that seven-figure milestone. I'd grown up with so many inspiring entrepreneurs around me, so I was excited to be following in their footsteps. I hoped they were proud of me.

One particular evening, I excitedly showed my 84-year-old grandpa my website. I pulled up iheartmylife.com and waited for a proud expression to come over his face. After all, he'd been an entrepreneur from a young age too, so I thought he'd be happy for me. However, I wasn't met with a smile, words of encouragement or anything promising; staring back at me was a blank face. He didn't get it and didn't know what to say. I was devastated; I ran upstairs crying and refused to talk to anyone. My grandpa left the house soon afterward, and James said he felt awful about the way he'd reacted. We've never talked about that moment.

Looking back I can see that of course my grandpa wasn't going to get it. He didn't even know how to use a computer! But I know firsthand that being a woman with big dreams in a world that often thinks small can be lonely at times. You wonder if there's something wrong with you; whether you should just be grateful for what you have. You question yourself and why you want more. Other people question you too. You want to fit in, but at the same time, you're wrestling with who you really are and what you know you're meant for.

I've had friendships fade away and end over the years. I've had negative comments emailed to me and written about me on Facebook. I've even experienced family members telling me I'm selfish and that all I care about is making money.

In working with clients all over the world, I've seen the reality of unsupportive friendships, spouses, and even parents, and I know how painful that can be. But I've also experienced the flipside – finally finding a tribe that gets you and forming new friendships and relationships that are grounded in support and encouragement.

If this is something you're longing for, stick with me. I'm going to show you how to handle those people in your life who don't get it, as well as create new relationships with people who do. The truth is, relationships are essential to your success, and you're not going to reach your goals without support in your life. That's ultimately what this chapter is about.

And rest assured I'm not going to suggest that you cut everyone out of your life. Instead, it's about taking a social inventory, so to speak, to ensure you really are setting yourself up for success. It's crucial to monitor who you're spending your time with, and choose wisely. Your job is not to change everyone's viewpoint – it's to stand true in what you know is right for you.

Those who are meant to stay in your life will rise up. Just like my grandpa. Since that Christmas, he has been incredibly supportive. He even told me recently that he sees me pushing around wheelbarrows of money. It just took him a while to 'get it' and that's okay. Remember, people can come back around too and those who love you will put in the effort to understand your dreams.

And those who are meant to fall away will fall away. The sooner you make peace with that, the better.

What Your Success Means to Others

As my business grew and I became more successful – and started talking about things like money mindset and the amount of money I was making – it made certain people in my life uncomfortable and challenged many of my relationships. After all, we're not supposed to talk about money, right?

In the minds of many of my closest friends and family members, I was no longer the same person. I was straying from the tribe, and, whether they knew it or not, that scared them. From an evolutionary perspective, when we step outside of the box and do things differently, it not only affects our own safety, it affects that of the rest of the tribe too. It makes others feel as if they don't know us anymore and thus can't trust us.

When you're not aligned with the vision others have for you, they become confused.

We have an inherent dislike of change (remember, the mind deems it unsafe), and when the people in your life don't know what sort of box to put you in, they feel uneasy and have a difficult time relating to you. You no longer equal 'safe.'

They also worry about what your success means *about them.* Think about it like this: what does it mean for the mother of the woman talking about making $50,000 a month? (Answer: it means she did something wrong while raising her daughter since she's now talking about money and appears to be greedy.) What does it mean for the woman whose best friend from high school has now 'made it'? (Answer: it means that she and her friend are now on different levels, and she's going to be forgotten; or that the now successful friend thinks she's 'better than' her.) These are just a few simple examples.

In her book *A Tribe Called Bliss*, Lori Harder says, 'Whether you realize it or not, if you have a tribe you most likely have an undisclosed agreement with some of them. It states in invisible ink that if you start to transcend, grow, or change your beliefs you will threaten your sense of belonging and will somehow be punished, made to feel foolish or make people feel bad.'[3]

But the thing is, when you have a growth mindset instead of a fixed mindset, it's inevitable that you'll be constantly changing. And for that reason, you aren't the same from year to year and will outgrow some of your 'past-life friends,' as I call them. And that's okay. This romantic notion that your best friends from childhood should remain your best friends forever is old school and is in fact a very rare scenario.

Just like the career path you chose at 18, you'll probably outgrow a lot of your relationships. But shouldn't that be the case? We're unique individuals with our own growth trajectories. I hope I'm not the same person at 40 that I was at 18. Don't you? I love what David Neagle says about this in his *The Successful Mind Podcast*, 'Some relationships are for a reason, some are for a season, and some are forever.'[4] And there's no need to make that wrong. It's just life.

Cut Ties

For that reason, there may come a time when, after all is said and done, you realize you have to cut ties with some of your family members or friends. Don't misunderstand me: you don't have to go on a culling rampage all at once, but I do want you to start paying attention to which relationships in your life are actually making you feel good and serving you. I also want you to start being unapologetic about what you need (and what you don't need) from your relationships.

For example, one of my former coaches, Marla Mattenson, said that when she was working on transforming her money story, she invited a friend over to her home, where she had her monetary goal and some money mantras taped to the wall. Her friend took one look at these and laughed in Marla's face. Her reaction? 'Get the fuck out of my house.'

Remember when I said that you don't have room for even one negative thought? Well, if there's someone in your life who is going to corrupt your vision, you need to be fiercely protective of your mind. And sometimes that means you'll be forced to cut certain people out of your life. That may seem harsh, but you need to start asking yourself what you're actually getting from your current relationships. If the answer is nada, maybe it's time to make that decision.

And if you're not in the place where you can be unapologetic about what you're not willing to hear, like my coach Marla (after all, she's quite the badass), decide who you *can* talk to about your dreams. If you're on the cusp of greatness and not as confident as you'd like to be, choose those people wisely, because in this period you're impressionable, and we don't want anyone coming in and infecting your positive mind and spirit. In other words, if your tribe isn't supportive of your dreams, get a new tribe. (Don't worry, I'll show you how!)

Find Your Tribe

With all this breaking of ties and crazy family rules, you may be wondering how in the world you can find people who *will* get you? When I first moved to London, I had no idea how to make friends. In fact, I decided online dating would be way easier than going to a bar and asking other women to be my friend.

As I've already shared, when I started my business, creating friendships wasn't even on my radar. I was so focused on building my business that I didn't even consider making it a priority. But as I invested in online group programs and masterminds, I naturally met people on the same wavelength and developed friendships.

The biggest factor in creating my new social network has been investing in my dreams.

I now have friends all around the world who are in alignment with my dreams and desires, and it's made all the difference. It's the same for many of my clients. I've been able to foster connections between them through my IHML programs – it's one of the things I've underestimated when it comes to accessing my impact. So many of my clients have made their new best friends through these groups; they came in for the content but they left with so much more. Plus, these relationships have helped them reach greater heights.

For example, in our groups, I encourage bragging, and jealousy is seen as a good thing – when you have that mindset and are surrounded by others who think similarly, anything is possible and you can go so much further. This pertains to financial success as well. When you see other women creating their 'new normal' financially, you believe you can do it too.

These relationships are possibility driven, and display that there's more than enough success to go around. We're all in this together, and another woman's success is also your success. When you operate with that belief, everything changes, including your relationships.

So, whether it's a mentor, a mastermind, an online group you connect with virtually, or a local entrepreneurs' club – *you* get to decide – making connections with like-minded people and

We're all in this together: another woman's success is also your success.

getting support is non-negotiable. Also, don't discount the power of the Universe in this area. If friendships are something you're craving, make it a priority and focus in your life and request the Universe to bring connections your way.

Connecting as an Introvert

One of my most successful clients posted this question in our Facebook group: 'Has anyone been to a blog conference before? There's one here in NYC tomorrow that I'm considering attending, but truth be told, even though I'm not shy, I'm an introvert and in-person events aren't always my thing! Does anyone have advice? Thanks in advance!' Ring a bell? It resonates with me too.

People who know me well probably realize that I'm not the biggest extrovert, and I'm not someone who loves spending lots of time in crowds – it can feel a bit exhausting and hasn't always been my favorite thing. Maybe you're also someone who's felt that traditional 'networking' can be a bit awkward and tiresome; or maybe the idea of going to a 1000-person conference makes you break into a cold sweat. I hear you. But there's some good news: you can make authentic connections in a way that's fun and natural. It just takes a mindset shift.

There are plenty of successful introverts out there: Elon Musk, Bill Gates, J.K. Rowling, Emma Watson.[5] Oprah Winfrey even admitted to being an introvert when she was interviewing the actress Amy Schumer on *Super Soul Sunday*.[6]

Over the past few years, I've learned that even as an introvert it's so important to show up and build new relationships if you want to achieve your goals quicker – and actually enjoy the process. There's a massive return on investment. After all, you're not going to change the world by just sitting behind your computer.

For example, just like the IHML Show opportunity, although I'd believed a book deal was in my future, it happened much more quickly due to my connections. That realization is what helped me shift my feelings about big groups, networking, and conferences away from a place of nervousness and dread. I began looking at these opportunities as a chance to find new, amazing business companions and confidants, and a way in which doors could open faster and the IHML movement could spread further.

This mindset shift has made a huge difference for me, and if you're struggling today with nervousness or dread when it comes to visibility or making new connections, then I encourage you to give it a try. The next time an opportunity to make new connections (or do an interview, etc.) arises, think about the amazing people out there who are waiting to meet you – to be your next big supporter, encourager, or promoter. Really give this mental exercise a chance – I'm confident you'll see a shift in how you feel.

Networking is not about mingling awkwardly in a room, or fumbling your way through a series of questions in an interview – it's about you finding your soulmates and showing the world the incredible gifts you have to offer! Doesn't it sound much more exciting not to be alone on this journey? There's power in numbers.

Celebration Break

You can make friends and connections even as an introvert! It's possible, and you're not meant to do this alone.

The Benefits of Having a Mentor

As you've probably realized, I've also had a different type of support throughout my entire success journey: mentorship and coaches. I knew very early on that the business guessing game wasn't one that I wanted to play. After all, that was the slow track to everything I so badly wanted.

If you're looking to fast-track your own success, I recommend you invest in a mentor. One of the main reasons to do this is for the belief they will have in you. Sometimes they can see potential that you didn't even realize was there. They can see the path because they are above the trees, with a clear vantage point, whereas right now, you're in the thick of the woods, fumbling your way through and not knowing how long it's going to take or if you're going to make it.

Why not reach out for guidance? It's a no-brainer when you think about it.

As Oprah Winfrey says, 'A mentor is someone who allows you to know that no matter how dark the night, in the morning, joy will come. A mentor is someone who allows you to see the higher part of yourself when sometimes it becomes hidden to your own view.'[7]

In early 2015, when I wanted my income to exceed six figures, I knew that, once again, I needed help getting there. After all, I didn't know how to reach that money milestone, and I wasn't about to try to figure it out myself.

I still remember the day my coach Gina DeVee, from the original group program I took part in, emailed me, asking if I'd like to be a part of her high-level coaching program. This was designed to support female entrepreneurs move from six to seven figures. It was a 12-month program that involved attending retreats in four exotic locations around the world – Bali, St. Tropez, LA and Florence.

I'd actually seen this opportunity in my inbox and on Facebook, but I'd quickly dismissed it as not meant for me. *Isn't this for women who are further along*? I thought. *Don't I have to be at least 30 years old to commit to something like this?* (It's amazing what our mind comes up with to keep us stuck!)

And then there was the money: the program cost $125,000. It was basically like buying a house. Even with the monthly installment payments, it would be a massive commitment, the likes of which I'd never experienced. But I was blown away that someone I admired so much in the industry wanted to work with me. And if she saw my potential and thought I could reach seven figures, maybe I could. I ended up saying yes, and that was just the start.

Invest in Your Own Success

To date I've invested more than $400,000 in my own success and business. Yes, that's the same as 30 mid-range cars, and 10 times what the average American makes in a year. But I've also made millions of dollars, transformed my life (and James's life), and had an impact in the world. Can you really put a price tag on that?

Yet I know that in this moment, investing in *your* success may seem like a scary thing. Maybe purchasing this book was a stretch. I hear you, but I also want you to go back to the Mindset chapter and recall that you always have enough money for all your desires. Remember, you can't want something without the solution to getting it also being there – *simultaneously*. They go hand in hand.

I'm not asking you to invest six figures or even $6 this second, but I *am* asking that you remain open-minded and keep everything you've learned thus far about possibility and wealth at the forefront.

My hope is that you'll start to see that holding yourself back from getting support isn't serving anyone. You have so much potential sitting there, ready to be brought to the surface. And if you have a business (or the dream of one), your lack of investment is definitely hindering your success in ways you might not have considered.

For example, how can you ask others to invest in you if you haven't invested in you? As author and lecturer Stuart Wilde says: 'The truth is that if you don't invest in yourself others pick up on that, and that, in itself, devalues what you are in their minds. Further, it is hard to ask others for their backing and support if you won't back yourself.'[8]

Take a look at the world of athletics. At no point do professional athletes fail to invest in their success and receive support. All the best athletes have at least one coach at their side, and often several. I've also seen firsthand that the top entrepreneurs tend to have a life coach, business coach, masseuse, personal trainer, and cook on hand – a whole network of support and specialists. We're not meant to do this alone. And if we're looking to do something big, it's not even an option.

So, why are we waiting until we reach the top to get the help we need? Let's take a look at what holds us back from investing in ourselves (in addition to the money), as well as why it's imperative to your success.

Independence

When James and I were dating, back in 2011, we naturally spoke about his past dating experience and the other women he'd met along the journey. During a few of our initial conversations, James shared with me that, especially when he moved to London, the type of woman he dated prided herself on being self-sufficient.

She wasn't quick to let anyone in, for fear of being hurt, and didn't want to 'need' anyone else. This wasn't exactly the type of woman James was looking for. Although he appreciated a strong woman, he didn't want to date someone with a wall up; he's a giving person and he wanted that to be valued.

I can relate to wearing self-reliance like a badge. I grew up the oldest of four kids, and although I had the best, most supportive and kind parents, I naturally learned to do quite a few things on my own and became really independent.

When I moved across the world to the UK by myself, that independence served me. Finding my first apartment was a struggle. I lived in a hotel for a while and then had to relocate to a hostel because I didn't have enough money to keep paying for the hotel. When I found an apartment, instead of paying for a taxi to move my stuff, I moved myself, walking 20 minutes across town on foot and up four flights of stairs with four jam-packed suitcases. I arrived a sweaty mess, but I did it.

So when I met James, asking for help wasn't exactly second nature; but at the same time, that didn't stop me from letting him in – which is where I think so many younger women are going wrong.

We're the generation of purpose, but also of 'I'll do it myself.'

We're not meant to do this alone. And if we're looking to do something big, it's not even an option.

And believe me, this attitude doesn't just apply to getting support professionally: it applies to every area of our lives. For example, on at least one of my coaching calls each month, there's someone who balks at my suggestion of getting help, especially around the house. My clients wonder if it makes them less of a woman not to clean the house or do the cooking or laundry. 'What would my mom think?' they ask. I say this with love and respect to you and them: You were not born just to clean toilets and die.

There's a fear of becoming too dependent, or of needing someone so much that if they ever leave or it doesn't work out, you'll end up stranded. And with the divorce rate so high, that mindset is easy to understand. But we're not talking about divorce here, and we're definitely not talking about you becoming Wonder Woman. I know it sounds really sexy to be able to say you did it all on your own, without any help, but it's *so not.* And the reality is that you can't do all the things on your own. And you shouldn't! That's the slow path to everything you're looking to achieve.

Worthiness

One of the other roadblocks to self-investment is feeling unworthy of it. Many clients come to me with that belief. They may not know that this is what's going on beneath the surface, but it's easy to spot the pattern.

Again, we're programmed to put others first. Make sure your kids have new clothes for school, that your husband gets the new golf clubs, that your mom has an incredible birthday – these are all very stereotypical examples (and important to a certain extent). But my point is, what about you? Is it time to think about what it's going to take for you to become the best version of you, and most importantly, to be happy? Aren't you worthy of your desires and the success you want? Weren't you born to shine?

It may take some practice, but you can start with small investments, like buying yourself flowers, getting the manicure, taking a bath. Maybe you can purchase one session with a mentor or attend a seminar? Or how about just giving the house cleaner a try? (I promise, you'll never go back!) You *are* worthy.

Success Tip

If you don't feel worthy of the support you're craving, practice flipping the switch on that thinking: I *am* worthy. I *am* worthy. I *am* worthy.

Trust

If you're resisting investing in your dreams, you also have to ask yourself whether one of the issues is that you don't actually trust yourself to make that money back or see a return. When I started my business, I distinctly remember seeing an interview with a financial advisor online in which he said the best thing you can do when you're starting out is invest in yourself – that's the only guaranteed investment with a positive result.

That was enough for me, and I haven't stopped investing. But for so many women, that self-belief isn't there, so they don't trust themselves or ever move forward. If that's you right now, ask yourself *what's blocking that self-belief?* What's stopping you from trusting that it'll work out?

I recently surveyed my audience and asked them, 'What do you believe will happen if you don't succeed'? Only one woman said that she doesn't have a belief like that, and is totally confident in her long-term success. In case you're curious, the other responses were:

- 'I'll have to go back to working in a 9–5 job.'
- 'I won't have the success to show for it, despite working hard.'
- 'I won't grow into the person I know I was created to be.'
- 'I will become deeply depressed, seeing others live their dreams.'
- 'I won't be able to put food on the table.'

What would it take for you to create a mindset that's *certain* of your success? You may not know exactly what it will look like, but how free would you feel with that certainty? How confident would you be when the time came to invest? That's what we want to create.

You 'Don't Have' the Money

Investing in yourself and your dreams isn't actually an alien concept for those of us living in the Western world. We do it all the time when we take out the student loan for that $30,000 per year university or we attend that seminar for work. Or think about medical school. That investment is around $300,000, and we all know the prestige that comes with that decision.

But especially when it comes to investing on a personal level, or on behalf of your own dreams – like starting a business – there's a disconnect. For some reason, it's still not as socially acceptable to take out a business loan, move forward by putting the first step on a credit card, or ask to borrow money from friends or family. But let's be real – getting a college education isn't necessarily a guarantee of success!

For that reason, the reality is that most of us don't have the money sitting under the mattress to fund our dreams, and because we freak out about borrowing it, those dreams never actually happen.

Take entrepreneurship for example, and let me paint you a picture. You want to have the ability to make more money and create your own schedule. You dream of starting a business so you can work for yourself. Right now, you're in a 9–5 job, just scraping by and living from paycheck to paycheck, so there isn't any extra at the end of the month, and you don't have any savings. You want to invest in getting the support you need to get started, yet you feel that you should have the money sitting there in a savings account in order to do so, because credit cards are bad, and you couldn't possibly take out a business loan.

So, year after year, you try to put money away to start the business, but between your rent, bills, and that occasional trip, you aren't able to save enough to get started. So you keep putting off your dreams, all the while continuing to tell yourself that you'll get started 'as soon as you have the money.' I hope you're starting to see how ridiculous that is. Why would you already have the money?

And by the way, we're not talking about a lot of money here. Let's use the online consulting/coaching industry as an example. In the beginning, you don't actually have much overhead besides a computer, website fees, and some marketing. You could start on $2,000 if you built your site yourself (and there's really no excuse not to these days, with all the template-based sites out there). Yet for so many of us, the idea of putting that on a credit card, or taking out a small loan, seems ridiculous. Yet we'll spend $100,000 on a college education. Are you seeing how backward this is?

Anyone Can Find the Money

I'm not saying there's anything wrong with getting an education – quite the opposite, actually – but why do we think we're done investing in ourselves after the age of 22? Isn't that when the magic really starts to happen? And with the pressure of the real world on our back, it actually becomes even more essential.

I hope you're getting this. You have to start operating with the belief that if the desire is there, so is the solution. When you show up in that way, doors will open, and you'll find the money.

My first investment was made on James's credit card. Amex literally helped fund my dreams for years. And that's not the only option; remember, anything is possible, and you always have enough money for your desires. And money miracles are possible! I had a call with a potential client who was a friend of a woman who sold her company for around $32 million. She saw how miserable her friend was in her 9–5 job and offered to give her money to leave and move forward in her own business. Are you starting to see what's possible?

What's It Costing You?

So far in this chapter, we've covered a few reasons why you may be hesitant to invest in your own success and get the support you need. There are many more that I see come up in my clients, but we don't need to go there. I don't want to continue to stay in that frame of mind; my purpose and mission is to support you in moving forward and that means getting out of that place. So, it's time to ask yourself this:

What's staying stuck or playing the success guessing game costing you? The answer is simple: your life.

The truth is, we're all self-medicating in some way or another. We don't want to feel pain. We don't want to dig up anything that may mean we're no longer safe. And that's how the ego views change – it's unsafe. So when someone suggests you go into therapy, work with a coach, or start a business, and they reach out their hand and offer to help you, it can be scary.

Yet how many of us are reaching out our hand every day to something that's not serving us – in the form of alcohol, endless spending on items we don't need, another scroll through Facebook, the trip that's meant to fix everything. We're not actually getting to the root of our unhappiness, anxiety or depression with those 'investments.'

Everything is an investment of our time, energy, attention, and sometimes, funds. Are you going to continue to mask the pain or desire, to quench it for a temporary period of time only to realize you're not actually happy or satisfied? Or are you going to get to the root of it and actually make a change? You have to ask yourself what's scarier: never going for your dreams and staying stuck in your current reality, or creating a new life for you and your family?

Let me give you another example. My client Jessica realized that not investing was costing her a whole lot more than moving forward and getting support. Every year for about a decade, she'd been going away on what she called her 'goal-planning weekends' to focus on setting goals for herself. But she came to realize that her goals were falling by the wayside and that she wasn't making progress toward her dreams.

She knew she couldn't keep waiting around for her goals to just happen (after all, she'd been doing the same goal-planning weekend for 10 years yet still felt stuck). She'd been in the I Heart My Life community for a while and heard about our program for new entrepreneurs but was really struggling with the decision to join. She thought, *I can't spend that much money on my dreams – it's too expensive. I could never do that!*

But then, in a moment of clarity, she thought, *What's it costing me not to do this?* And *that* is the question I want to encourage you to consider today. What is it costing you not to get the help you need? It could be costing you your happiness, fulfillment, financial stability, your family's future, your confidence. It could be costing you trips around the world to amazing places, or the freedom to live life on your terms. Simply put, it could be costing you your life.

Action Step

Where in your life do you know you need support or more connection? Brainstorm all the ways in which you could make that happen this week, and then take action on one of those ways.

CHAPTER 11

Success

'Your job is not to say "how," it's to say "yes."'[1]

DR. WAYNE W. DYER

In March 2018, I was in a taxi on my way to a meeting in Notting Hill, sending emails as we drove along. The driver started to cut through the back streets of Kensington, and I looked up from my iPhone at the perfect moment and realized where I was: the street I'd lived on when I'd moved to the city eight years earlier. I was shocked. I hadn't been to the area for years, and to be on that very street, on that very day, couldn't have been a fluke.

This was where, in my closet-size apartment, I'd cried, wishing for my life to get good. This is where someone literally threw up out the window and it blew in and landed on my bedspread. This is where I came home after my first date with James. This is where I got deathly ill (at least that's how it felt) when I caught the flu from Edison, the little boy I took care of as a nanny. This is where I wrote that letter to myself. All those thoughts ran through my mind.

This time, I didn't try to hide those tears rolling down my cheeks with the realization that I'd literally come full circle. I'd arrived in London with the dream of writing a book, and the reason I was going to Notting Hill was to meet the team at Hay House UK to discuss a deal for the very book that's in your hands today.

Everything that I'd been intending, wishing, hoping for all my life had come true. James and I went to the top of the Eiffel Tower. I'd found my purpose. I'd surpassed my financial goals. It had all happened. And it continues to do so.

A few months later, I followed my heart and desires and traveled to Florence to start this book. On day five of my trip, I ate my five croissants at breakfast (I'm not joking – in Italy I have the amazing ability to eat a ton of food and only gain a few pounds due to all the steps that exist everywhere, so I go for it!) and afterward, I moved to a separate area in front of the Four Seasons hotel to start writing.

About 30 minutes in, a harpist started playing for the guests who were still enjoying breakfast. A harpist! I looked over at her and my eyes welled up. This is what life is about, I thought. Those pinch-me moments that take your breath away. Those moments when you realize that actually, there isn't much that truly matters in the world: just people, your health, and moments like this. Writing your first published book while overlooking Florence's Duomo.

What it evoked in me was massive gratitude for my past decisions and everything that had led me to that moment. It was true validation that the magic lies in following your heart and your desires.

> *After all, just a few years earlier, I'd been that girl arriving in London with four suitcases and a dream. She'd wanted to write a book. She'd been dreaming of moments like this. Somehow she always knew they were possible, and never lost hope.*

Whether my story resonates with you because you've experienced your own full-circle moment or because you have the dream of a moment like that, this chapter is about putting together all you've learned in this book so you have a full picture of how to create the life and success you're craving.

We've covered so much, but there are some final pieces I want you to really understand. So open your heart, and let's take this final step together.

Create the Epic Motion Picture That's Your Life

When I launched the IHML Show in January 2018, my first guest was my former coach Dr. James Rouse. In the episode, he opened up by asking my listeners to consider this question: 'Are you living the epic motion picture that is your life?'

The epic motion picture.

I don't know about you, but I'd never thought about my life in that way. But it's true – this life is your epic motion picture, and you're the Director and Leading Lady. At least that's how it's supposed to be. You're meant to have pinch-me moments and harpists at breakfast and experiences that take your breath away. You're meant to come full circle. Yet, so many of us are living a life that doesn't resemble what we desire.

I know that if you're here with me today, you want to change that current reality. Here are some final tips for making that change…

Are You Under-Living?

Although today he has the power to make you cry just by being in his mere presence, Dr. James Rouse didn't always show up that way in the world. On my show, he told the story of living a life of mediocrity, until the day he got a wakeup call from his very own Earth Angel.

As a young man, Dr. James used to work into the night at a truck stop as a gas station attendant. He said he would run out to the trucks that pulled up to the fuel stop, give each driver a great big smile, and ask them, 'How can I serve you?'

One day in particular, a truck pulled in, and at first, the driver didn't utter a word upon hearing the young man's greeting. He just looked at him in a way that no one else had; he looked right *through* him, and said, 'I don't know what it is that you think you're doing here, but I'm going to Boston and then I'm going to turn around and come back through New York tomorrow night. If I see you here when I come back through in 24 hours, I'm going to kick your ass.'

Dr. James had never seen this man before, but he said that in that moment, he knew what he had seen in him. After all, it was the same thing that he wanted to believe was true about himself. For years, he had heard, 'You do not belong here. You belong doing something much greater than this.' It was time to say 'yes' to that calling, so he took that prayer and invocation and ran with it and applied to college the very next day. Thirteen years later, he became a doctor.

For me, Dr. James's story is a powerful reminder that so many of us are under-living. We're in jobs we hate; we dread waking up each morning; we're asleep at the wheel of life. Ask yourself today: are you where you belong? Or are you meant to be doing something much greater than this? Are you under-living your life? If so, know that I see possibility in you. I see opportunity. I see success. And if I see you in the same place tomorrow as you are today, I too, am going to (lovingly) kick your booty.

Success Tip

Take a few minutes to reflect on Dr. James's story. Write down how it made you feel and what it brought up for you.

This is Your Journey

I need you to always remember that this is *your* journey. No one else gets to make the rules. You are in charge here. It's time to throw the Reality Rulebook out the window. You know, *this* book:

Do well in school. (After all, it's your job until you have a job, and if you can't do that, well, you're failing at life.)

Get into a good college.

Study hard, and don't party too much.

Shadow people who have the career you want, and make connections.

Get an internship.

Apply for the jobs before your graduate.

Land the best job you can find.

Get an apartment.

Buy work clothes (man, I hate work clothes).

Date.

Get married.

Have kids.

Be a good daughter, sister, mother, wife.

Take two trips a year (if you're lucky).

The end.

You're meant for so much more. As Oprah says, 'Create the highest, grandest vision possible for your life, because you become what you believe.'[2] This is your one life, and you create your own version of realistic.

This is your one life, and you create your own version of realistic.

Expect Everything to Be Yours

It's not enough for you to desire something: you need to *expect* it to be on its way. You have to really, truly know that it's about to manifest into your life. This is the difference between *wanting* true love and *expecting* it. Expecting is much stronger, isn't it?

What would it look like if you expected the raise? What if you expected to meet your future husband? Expected to lose the weight? Expected to become a millionaire? This is another emotion that needs to be generated by you – you won't naturally expect your dreams to be a reality, like you expect to take your next breath. It's not yet ingrained, but it can be with practice.

Also note that when you do start to practice thinking in this way, your mind will fight you. After all, is it really 'safe' to expect to be successful? The mind will say things like, *But what if you fail? What if people laugh at you? What if it doesn't work out*? As my friend Susie Moore would say, 'What if it does work out?[3]

When you start to operate from a place of it already having happened, everything will start to change, and expectation gets you into that state.

Follow the Signs and Angels

In those moments of disbelief, doubt or confusion, continue to trust your heart, make your decisions right, and look for the signs. There will be so many signs if you're open to them. For example, in Florence, my sign came with the pizza, with a lot of progress made on my book, with how I felt when I enjoyed a gorgeous Italian coffee on the hotel terrace, when I got to look out at the Duomo and think about all the incredible artists who had also been inspired by this city – Michelangelo, Leonardo, Botticelli. There are signs and angels all around you that are telling you you're on the right path. Follow them.

For Dr. James, that man at the truck stop was an angel. Angels can be the people out there pushing you, knowing that you can do more with your life; and on the flip side, they can be those who are telling you can't do something. *Both* are angels. Both can help you move forward and inspire you to allow yourself to become who you're meant to be. What are your angels telling you? Are you ready to finally listen?

Remember What Got You Here

What got you here won't be the thing that takes you there, right? There's validity to that statement, but please know that what you possess inside, what you've always possessed, is the great ability to make things happen. I guarantee there are qualities within you that already make you poised for great success.

For example, if you look back at your life, or even the last year, what has gotten you to this point? What has resulted in success for you? What has enabled you to have this book in your hands, to go for new opportunities, to show up on behalf of your dreams?

Whatever the answer is for you – maybe a personality trait or faith – keep doing it, and leave the rest behind you. Let your past give you clues about what's required from you to make your future dreams a reality. You already have so many incredible qualities to draw upon.

> **Success Tip**
>
> Make a list of all the qualities, decisions, and ways in which you've shown up that have served you and your success.

Say 'Yes' to Opportunities

'Yes.' It's a simple word. It has the power to change everything though. 'Yes' to a proposal means you've found the person you want to spend forever with. 'Yes' to the job means you'll spend 10,000 hours a year doing that work – probably more since 9–5 isn't really a thing anymore.

However, I find that when it comes to our dreams, we say 'no' far more than 'yes' due to fear or uncertainty. Saying yes is one of the reasons why I am where I am today. The truth is, most of us *are* scared to follow our dreams. It *isn't* always easy. There *are* moments on the path to creating your dreams when you do have to step outside of your comfort zone. You have to keep saying yes to get what it is that you want, despite the fear, insecurity, lack of confidence, or anything else that creeps up.

Frankly, when I look back at everything I've done over the last eight years, I don't actually know how I did most of it. But just like me, you're far more capable than you know, and you will figure it out. Even if you don't feel ready, know that you can (and should) still start today. You have the capability to achieve your dreams. It's there inside of you.

Even a small action is better than no action at all. So if you're feeling stuck in a rut, take action. Learn something. Try something new. Put yourself out there. There's no better time than now to start truly embracing your potential and pursuing your passions. There's no reason to put your desires on hold any longer. After all, one small step can be all it takes to start walking in the direction of your dreams.

You Don't Have to Do Everything

On the flip side, hear me when I say that you don't have to do all the things this second. In fact, you shouldn't.

As driven women, we are multi-passionate and we have new ideas every day. We experience 'shiny object syndrome' and always want to reach for the next thing. Focus on what's important to you right now. That's the action that's going to create the most leverage for you. You *don't* have four months left to live: you have time. Manage your energy.

From My Little Girl to Yours

In those moments when I passed my first flat in London and was writing my book in Italy, I thought about my little girl. The little girl inside all of us. The Emily who played with her Barbies and dreamt of her own Ken to ride away with in the convertible.

The Emily who tried so hard in school. The Emily who beat herself up when she didn't get that perfect score. The Emily who lived in a hostel when she moved to London. The Emily who went on all those blind dates, hoping to find 'the one.' The Emily who was a nanny for a while. She'd come so far. She'd be so proud of me. I had to make sure to remember that and think of her more often, even though it wasn't natural to do so.

Those of us who are driven, and well versed in achieving, often forget the incredible things we've already done and how far we've come.

What about your own little girl? What would she say to you? Picture her walking up to you and looking at you lovingly. I see her wrapping her arms around you, telling you how well you're doing. What a special person you are. How cool you are. How she only wishes she could be like you someday. She could never have envisioned this.

In those moments, take it in. Express gratitude for your little girl. After all, she got you to this place. She's incredible, and she's still a big part of you. Channel your little girl when it feels like you're not good enough, that you can't do it, that you don't have the answers, that no one likes you – she believes in you with every ounce of her being. She thinks you're amazing. She wants to be you when she grows up. Use her admiration – take it in. Allow it to remind you that the sky is the limit when it comes to your dreams. Dream. Dream. Dream.

Life doesn't have to be difficult. You can spend time lying on the grass, looking at dandelions. You can continue to dream of true love. You can be that astronaut, actress, or whatever you want to be. You get to decide. How does your little girl want you to show up? What decisions does she want you to make right now? What would make her even more proud? In what ways can you channel her wisdom, youth, vibrancy, zest for life? She's there if you need her.

Sometimes, in those moments when I'm taking life too seriously, overcomplicating things or looking to make a decision, I also channel the woman I'll be one day. I think about her and her wisdom – all she's been through. I know even now, when I look back and think about all I've done up to this point, there's only one thing I'd do differently: worry less. When you're in your 80s or 90s, nearing the end of your life, you're going to regret those precious moments you spent worrying. Because you were actually in the right place at the right time. Everything was working out as it was meant to.

Right now in this moment, what does that intelligent older version of you have to say? My guess is that she's so happy about the life you're living, but she wants you to remember not to take a single day for granted. She encourages you to take more chances, to love harder, to experience more of those once-in-a-lifetime moments that deserve every ounce of your attention. She knows what you're capable of and invites you to raise the bar. To impact the world. To live life to the fullest and remember you have extraordinary gifts.

I can see her smiling softly at you, saying that you're doing a great job, and you don't have to worry – you have everything it takes. She tells you to trust that everything will work out. It's all going to come full circle. And when it comes down to it, all that matters is that you're living a life you love. Nothing else.

One More Thing Before You Go

You should know one more thing about me before we part ways: I've never liked surprises. My parents threw me a surprise 16th birthday party and invited my whole class – they told me I was going out to dinner with my mom and my best friend and her mom.

Although I was grateful they'd been so thoughtful (and frankly I couldn't believe they'd pulled it off), I was devastated because I wasn't wearing the right outfit. Because of that, I wasn't fully there. I wasn't fully myself. I didn't feel good enough. I didn't truly enjoy the moment. I wasn't present to my life that day. The one and only time I'd turn 16.

This is still something I'm overcoming: this element of not being present. Worrying about what people will think.

Wondering if I'm good enough. In my own head. Avoiding the element of surprise.

Why am I telling you this today? Why am I spending our last few moments admitting this struggle? I'm telling you as a matter of urgency. I'm sharing this because I want you to be present to this one life that you've been gifted. Don't you dare allow yourself to say 'I missed it,' 'I didn't really show up,' or 'I played it safe.'

You now have all the tools you need to create your something big. It may not be an easy journey, but there's nothing you can't handle. After all, you now have the recipe for success:

- Create self-belief.
- Remember that anything is possible.
- Listen to your heart above all else.
- Find your purpose, and trust that clarity is on its way.
- Transform your mindset.
- Set clear goals.
- Show up. (Show up big time.)
- Love yourself above all else.
- Appreciate challenge.
- Get support.
- Celebrate your success like your life depends on it.

Those are the steps I've used time and time again over the past few years to create a life that's better than my dreams. Was it perfect? No. Were there days when I wanted to cry (and did)? Totally. Did my ego come up full force? Of course. And it will for you too. Was I scared? Every second. But that's okay. That's how it's supposed to feel.

Trust, access faith you didn't know existed, lean on your little girl and wise older soul, take more action than ever before, move past your fears – and know that when you do, you'll be wildly surprised by how incredible your life turns out.

And, Lovely, in case it's still not obvious, you have everything you already need within. After all, it's never about the outfit.

Action Step

Think about the woman you were when you started this book, compared to who you are now that we've ended this journey together. Celebrate how far you've come and all you've accomplished. Channel your little girl and future self and journal on the thoughts and emotions that come up for you. And for goodness' sake, go have a glass of champagne!

Afterword

September 25, 2018

Dear Lovely ____________________,

I'm up at 5:10 a.m. writing you this letter – nearly eight years to the day since I wrote that letter to myself, the one in the Preface to this book. I'm in my kitchen in London; it's a new kitchen, but no less tied to my heart than the one in which I started my business years ago. I have a candle lit for us – to celebrate the end of our journey together.

But the truth is, it's just the start for you. What happens after you close this book is more important than our time together has been.

Continue to go back to the words you've read in this book. Continue to reread the chapters. Study everything that I've provided you with. Take it in. And implement all the Action Steps.

As you do so, pay attention to the shifts that start to occur. They may be simple at first – you get a new idea, someone calls you out of the blue, an opportunity appears as if out of nowhere – but just like getting that plane off the ground, things are about to pick up. You're about to soar, so hold on tight.

Trust that everything you want, wants you back. You don't have to worry. It's all there for the taking. Your life is there for the taking. It's all happening as it's meant to. You've always been in the right place at the right time, and today's no different. Nothing has been or ever will be an accident. Follow your heart. And know that I can't wait to see you shine.

Emily xx

Connect with Me

 iheartmylife.com

 iheartmylifenow

 @iheartmylifenow

References

Epigraph

1. Berhrand, G., 2013. *Your Invisible Power*. Merchant Books.

Introduction

1. OWN, 2011. 'Oprah's Belief in Herself in Yourself'. Available at: <www.youtube.com/watch?v=G1mPB5SJaEU> [accessed September 22, 2018].
2. Williamson, M., 2012. *The Law of Divine Compensation*. HarperOne.
3. Burchard, B., 2016. Available at: <www.twitter.com/BrendonBurchard/status/701555535305433094> [accessed September 22, 2018].
4. Robbins, M., 2017. *The 5 Second Rule*. Post Hill Press.
5. Acharya, S., Shukla, S. 'Mirror neurons: Enigma of the metaphysical modular brain,' *Journal of Natural Science, Biology and Medicine*. Available at: <www.ncbi.nlm.nih.gov/pmc/articles/PMC3510904> [accessed September 22, 2018].
6. Pidgeon, N., 2017. *Now Is Your Chance*. Hay House UK.
7. Schucman, H., 2008. *A Course in Miracles*. Foundation for Inner Peace.

Chapter 1: Belief

1. Winfrey, O., 1997. Graduate commencement address at Wellesley College, Boston.
2. Schucman, H., 2008. *A Course in Miracles*. Foundation for Inner Peace.

3. Williamson, M., 2012. *The Law of Divine Compensation*. HarperOne.
4. Campbell, R., 2015. *Light Is the New Black*. Hay House UK.

Chapter 2: Possibility

1. Gilbert, E., 2015. *Big Magic*. Bloomsbury Publishing.
2. Weller, C., 2017. 'There Are 36 Million Millionaires in the World and They Own Nearly Half the Planet's Wealth'. Available at: <www.inc.com/business-insider/36-million-millionaires-in-the-world-hold-46-percent-wealth-credit-suisse-global-wealth-report-2017.html> [accessed September 22, 2018].
3. Mason, N. and Richmond, C., 2018. 'Sir Roger Bannister obituary'. Available at: <https://www.theguardian.com/sport/2018/mar/04/sir-roger-bannister-obituary> [accessed September 22, 2018].
4. Viereck, G. S., 1929. 'What Life Means to Einstein'. Available at: <www.saturdayeveningpost.com/wp-content/uploads/satevepost/einstein.pdf> [accessed September 22, 2018].
5. Dyer, W., 2012. *Wishes Fulfilled.* Hay House, Inc.
6. O'Neill, J., 2013. *Universal Laws*. CreateSpace Independent Publishing Platform.
7. Hurst, K. 'Understanding and Applying The Law of Polarity (& The Secret Ritual)'. Available at: <www.thelawofattraction.com/understanding-applying-law-polarity-secret-ritual/> [accessed September 22, 2018].
8. Sharma, R. '*The Hero Within You Playbook*'. Available at: <www.robinsharma.com/lm/wp-content/uploads/2016/09/The-Hero-Within-You.pdf> [accessed September 22, 2018].
9. Edgley, R., 2018. 'World's Fittest Strongman'. Available at: <https://www.youtube.com/watch?v=BOVuaUjhvUY&feature=youtu.be> [accessed September 22, 2018].
10. ibid.
11. Dyer, W., 2012. *Wishes Fulfilled.* Hay House, Inc.

Chapter 3: Desire

1. LaPorte, D., 2014. *The Desire Map.* Sounds True.
2. Bassols, J., 2018. 'How to Start Thinking with the Heart'. Available at: <https://upliftconnect.com/how-to-start-thinking-with-the-heart/> [accessed September 22, 2018].
3. Harv Eker, T., 2005. *Secrets of the Millionaire Mind.* HarperBusiness.
4. Berhrand, G., 2013. *Your Invisible Power*. Merchant Books.
5. Gilbert, E., 2006. *Eat, Pray, Love*. Bloomsbury Publishing.
6. LaPorte, D., 2014. *The Desire Map.* Sounds True.

Chapter 4: Purpose

1. Forleo, M., 2015. www.facebook.com. <www.facebook.com/marieforleo/posts/the-world-needs-that-special-gift-that-only-you-have-love-the-idea-but-dont-know/10152896126183978/> [accessed September 22, 2018].
2. Schwartz, B., 20014. *The Paradox of Choice.* Harper Perennial.
3. Kagan, N., 2014. 'The Lively Show: Intentions, Values, And Meaning With Noah Kagan'. Available at: <http://jesslively.com/noahkagan/> [accessed September 22, 2018].
4. LaPorte, D., 2015. *The Fire Starter Sessions*. Harmony.
5. Forleo, M. 'Why You'll Never Find Your Passion'. Available at: <https://www.marieforleo.com/2014/04/find-your-passion> [accessed September 22, 2018].
6. Hicks, E. and Hicks, J., 2008. *Money and the Law of Attraction.* Hay House, Inc.

Chapter 5: Mindset

1. Harv Eker, T., 2005. *Secrets of the Millionaire Mind.* HarperBusiness.
2. Dooley, M., 2013. *Leveraging the Universe.* Atria Books/Beyond Words.
3. Harv Eker, T., 2005. *Secrets of the Millionaire Mind.* HarperBusiness.

4. Neagle, D., 2018. *The Successful Mind Podcast*; Episode 024: 'Why We Stop'. Available at: <www.podbean.com/media/share/dir-fikkt-465211e> [accessed September 22, 2018].

5. Harv Eker, T., 2005. *Secrets of the Millionaire Mind.* HarperBusiness.

6. Dweck, C., 2006. *Mindset.* Random House.

7. Siebold, S., 2010. *How Rich People Think.* London House Press.

8. Sharma, R. S., 2015. *The Monk Who Sold His Ferrari.* Harper Thorsons.

9. Hendricks, G., 2010. *The Big Leap.* HarperOne.

10. Definition of 'hopefully'. Available at: <https://en.oxforddictionaries.com/thesaurus/hopefully> [accessed September 22, 2018].

11. Lori Ansbach Eckert, The College at Brockport: State University of New York, 'The Effects of Mental Imagery on Free row Performance'. Available at: <https://digitalcommons.brockport.edu/cgi/viewcontent.cgi?article=1002&context=pes_theses,> [accessed September 22, 2018].

12. Gilbert, E., 2015. *Big Magic*. Bloomsbury Publishing.

13. Hendricks, G., 2010. *The Big Leap.* HarperOne.

14. Gilbert, E., 2015. *Big Magic*. Bloomsbury Publishing.

Chapter 6: Goals

1. Tracy, B., 2010. *No Excuses!* Vanguard Press.

2. Pritchett, P., 1994. *You*^{2} Pritchett & Associates.

3. Sharma, R., 2015. 'The 26 Titan Principles'. Available at : <https://medium.com/@robinsharma/the-26-titan-principles-52fc343332e6> [accessed September 22, 2018].

Chapter 7: Action

1. Dooley, M., 2018. 'Notes from the Universe'. Available at: <https://www.tut.com/other/noteshare/id/660/?noPopup=1> [accessed September 22, 2018].

2. Definition of 'pipe dream'. Available at <www.urbandictionary.com/define.php?term=pipe%20dream> [accessed September 22, 2018].

3. Robbins, M., 2012. *Stop Saying You're Fine*. Three Rivers Press.

4. Burchard, B., 2017. *High Performance Habits.* Hay House, Inc.

5. Kay, K. and Shipman, C., 2014. *The Atlantic:* 'The Confidence Gap' Available at: <https://www.theatlantic.com/magazine/archive/2014/05/the-confidence-gap/359815/> [accessed September 22, 2018].

6. Ibid.

7. Vanzant, I., 2015. *Trust.* Hay House, Inc.

8. Hill, N., 1937. *Think and Grow Rich.* Napoleon Hill Foundation.

9. Sharma, R. 'Robin Sharma's 5 Rituals that Predict Success'. Available at: <https://awakenthegreatnesswithin.com/robin-sharmas-5-rituals-that-predict-success/> [accessed September 22, 2018].

10. Nielsen, 2018. 'Time Flies: US Adults Now Spend Nearly Half a Day Interacting with Media, Available at: <www.nielsen.com/us/en/insights/news/2018/time-flies-us-adults-now-spend-nearly-half-a-day-interacting-with-media.html> [accessed September 22, 2018].

Chapter 8: Self

1. Lucille Ball, television actress, comedian (1911–1989).

2. The Dalai Lama, 2009. Vancouver Peace Summit, Canada.

3. McAndrew, F. T. 2016. 'Don't try to be happy. We're programmed to be dissatisfied'. Available at: <www.theguardian.com/commentisfree/2016/aug/17/psychology-happiness-contentment-humans-aspire-goals-accomplish-evolution> [accessed September 22, 2018].

4. Siebold, S. 2010. *How Rich People Think*, London House Press.

5. Burchard, B., 2017. *High Performance Habits.* Hay House, Inc.

6. Sharma, S., 2017. 'The 49 Best Lessons 2017 Taught Me'. Available at: <www.robinsharma.com/article/the-49-best-lessons-2017-taught-me> [accessed September 22, 2018].

7. LaPorte, D., 2017. *White Hot Truth*. Virtuonica

8. Winfrey, O., 2014. *What I Know for Sure*. Macmillan.

Chapter 9: Challenge

1. Hill, N., 1937. *Think and Grow Rich*. Napoleon Hill Foundation.

2. Lowry, V., 2004. 'Work out Now, Ache Later: How your Muscles Pay you Back'. Available at: <https://nytimes.com/2004/11/16/health/nutrition/work-out-now-ache-later-how-your-muscles-pay-you-back.html> [accessed September 22, 2018].

3. Vanzant, I., 2015. *Trust.* Hay House, Inc.

4. Hill, N., 2017. *Grow Rich! With Peace of Mind*. www.bnpublishing.com.

5. Sharma, R. 'My 20 Best Quotes for Epic Achievement'. Available at: <www.robinsharma.com/article/my-20-best-quotes-for-epic-achievement> [accessed September 22, 2018].

6. Vanzant, I., 2015. *Trust.* Hay House, Inc.

7. Winfrey, O., 2012. 'What Oprah Knows for Sure About Gratitude'. www.oprah.com Available at: <www.oprah.com/spirit/oprahs-gratitude-journal-oprah-on-gratitude> [accessed September 22, 2018].

Chapter 10: Support

1. Sharma, R., 2017. www.facebook.com. Available at: <www.facebook.com/RobinSharmaOfficial/videos/vb.105875750039/10155832205835040/?type=2&theater> [accessed September 22, 2018].

2. Higgs, S., 2015. 'Social norms and their influence on eating behaviours'. Available at: <www.sciencedirect.com/science/article/pii/S0195666314005017> [accessed September 22, 2018].

3. Harder, L., 2018. *A Tribe Called Bliss.* Gallery Books.
4. Neagle, D., 2018. *The Successful Mind Podcast*; Episode 028: 'Uncommon Ground'. Available at: <www.podbean.com /media/share/dir-4z3f3-49263b7> [accessed September 22, 2018].
5. Rampton, J., 2015. '23 of the Most Amazingly Successful Introverts in History'. Available at: <www.inc.com/john-rampton/23-amazingly-successful-introverts-throughout-history.html> [accessed September 22, 2018].
6. Winfrey, O., 2018. 'Oprah and Amy Schumer on Being Secret Introverts'. Available at: <www.youtube.com /watch?v=lcqAisTrCE8> [accessed September 22, 2018].
7. From an interview with Oprah Winfrey. Boston, January 13, 2002. WCVB-TV 5 News *CityLine.*
8. Wilde, S., 1995. *The Secret to Having Money Is Having Some*, Hay House, Inc.

Chapter 11: Success

1. Dyer, W., 2004. *The Power of Intention.* Hay House, Inc.
2. Winfrey, O., 2012. '7 Pieces of Wisdom from Oprah Winfrey (video)'. Available at: <www.guidedmind.com/blog/7-pieces-of-wisdom-from-oprah-winfrey> [accessed September 22, 2018].
3. Moore, S., 2016. *What If It Does Work Out?* CreateSpace Independent Publishing Platform.

Recommended Reading

As a child, I would read incessantly, but after college, for some reason I stopped. I guess life got in the way, and I didn't think I had the time. Maybe you're the same. If so, this is an opportunity to reignite your passion for books!

On my own journey to discovering my something big, transforming my life and achieving new levels of success, books have been essential to the results I've seen. As a successful woman, learning is non-negotiable. It's part of the recipe.

For that reason, I've listed below some books that I recommend you dive into, study, and use to further facilitate your own journey to everything you desire and more!

The Big Leap: Conquer Your Hidden Fear and Take Life to the Next Level, Gay Hendricks, HarperOne, 2010

How Rich People Think, Steve Siebold, London House Press, 2010

Secrets of the Millionaire Mind: Mastering the Inner Game of Wealth, T. Harv Eker, HarperCollins Publishers Ltd., 2005

Think and Grow Rich, Napoleon Hill, Napoleon Hill Foundation, 1937

The Science of Getting Rich, Wallace D. Wattles, Simon & Brown, 2013

The Desire Map: A Guide to Creating Goals with Soul, Danielle LaPorte, Sounds True, 2014

Trust: Mastering the 4 Essential Trusts: Trust in God, Trust in Yourself, Trust in Others, Trust in Life, Iyanla Vanzant, Hay House, Inc., 2015

Big Magic: Creative Living Beyond Fear, Elizabeth Gilbert, Bloomsbury Publishing, 2015

ABOUT THE AUTHOR

Wendy Yalom

Emily Williams is a success coach, entrepreneur, and author with a seven-figure business who, at one point, couldn't get a job at Starbucks.

After experiencing a quarter-life crisis, she moved from Ohio to London (where she knew no one!) and in 2014 launched her business, I Heart My Life. She made $442 in her first month – and then went on to hit six figures in six months, before her 30th birthday. She grew it to seven figures in under 18 months.

Today, she works with female entrepreneurs all over the world, helping them bust through the obstacles that hold their dreams and goals hostage so they can free themselves to live the lives they want, build their own online business, and hit their money goals. She's been featured in *Money*, *Entrepreneur*, *Business Insider*, *Forbes* and *Success* magazines.

Emily works with the love of her life, James, who is a High Performance Coach in I Heart My Life. They have a gorgeous cat named Lola.

iheartmylifenow

@iheartmylifenow

www.iheartmylife.com

Hay House Podcasts

Bring Fresh, Free Inspiration Each Week!

Hay House proudly offers a selection of life-changing audio content via our most popular podcasts!

Hay House Meditations Podcast

Features your favorite Hay House authors guiding you through meditations designed to help you relax and rejuvenate. Take their words into your soul and cruise through the week!

Dr. Wayne W. Dyer Podcast

Discover the timeless wisdom of Dr. Wayne W. Dyer, world-renowned spiritual teacher and affectionately known as "the father of motivation." Each week brings some of the best selections from the 10-year span of Dr. Dyer's talk show on HayHouseRadio.com.

Hay House World Summit Podcast

Over 1 million people from 217 countries and territories participate in the massive online event known as the Hay House World Summit. This podcast offers weekly mini-lessons from World Summits past as a taste of what you can hear during the annual event, which occurs each May.

Hay House Radio Podcast

Listen to some of the best moments from HayHouseRadio.com, featuring expert authors such as Dr. Christiane Northrup, Anthony William, Caroline Myss, James Van Praagh, and Doreen Virtue discussing topics such as health, self-healing, motivation, spirituality, positive psychology, and personal development.

Hay House Live Podcast

Enjoy a selection of insightful and inspiring lectures from Hay House Live, an exciting event series that features Hay House authors and leading experts in the fields of alternative health, nutrition, intuitive medicine, success, and more! Feel the electricity of our authors engaging with a live audience, and get motivated to live your best life possible!

Find Hay House podcasts on iTunes, or visit www.HayHouse.com/podcasts for more info.

HAY HOUSE

Online Video Courses

Your journey to a better life starts with figuring out which path is best for you. Hay House Online Courses provide guidance in mental and physical health, personal finance, telling your unique story, and so much more!

LEARN HOW TO:

- choose your words and actions wisely so you can tap into life's magic
- clear the energy in yourself and your environments for improved clarity, peace, and joy
- forgive, visualize, and trust in order to create a life of authenticity and abundance
- break free from the grip of narcissists and other energy vampires in your life
- sculpt your platform and your message so you get noticed by a publisher
- use the creative power of the quantum realm to create health and well-being

To find the guide for your journey, visit www.HayHouseU.com.

HAY HOUSE

Look within

Join the conversation about latest products,
events, exclusive offers and more.

Hay House UK

@HayHouseUK

@hayhouseuk

healyourlife.com

We'd love to hear from you!